As it is in Heaven

Seven Core Values of a Revival Culture

Ian Carroll

As It Is In Heaven: Seven Core Values of a Revival Culture

Copyright © 2016 by Ian Carroll Ministries

All rights reserved. No part of this book may be reproduced or transmitted in any form or by any means without written permission from the author.

ISBN (978-0-9982644-0-0)

Unless otherwise identified, all Scripture in this publication are from the NEW AMERICAN STANDARD BIBLE ©, The Lockman Foundation 1960, 1962, 1963, 1968, 1971, 1972, 1973, 1975, 1977, 1995. Used by permission. Other versions used include the Holy Bible: New International Version® (NIV®). Copyright © 1973, 1978, 1984, 2011 by International Bible Society. Used by permission of Zondervan Publishing House. All rights reserved; THE MESSAGE. Copyright © 1993, 1994, 1995, 1996, 2000, 2001, 2002.Used by permission of NavPress Publishing Group

Please note that the author's publishing style capitalizes certain pronouns in Scripture that refer to Father, Son, and Holy Spirit and may differ from other publishers' styles.

Dedication

This book is dedicated to everyone at Greater Chicago Church—the most encouraging, Kingdom-minded people I have ever met. Thank you for your continued perseverance to see the kingdom of this world become the Kingdom of our Lord and of His Christ.

To my leadership team, JD and Carrie Leman, Jamie Cleghorn, Heather Treadway, and Bam and Liz Stanton, thank you.

Special thanks to Melissa Amato and Julia Kelly Smith for all the hard work editing and making me look like a genius!

Finally, to my sweetheart, my best friend, and my wife, Rachel, I don't know what I would do without you.

Table of Contents

Endorsements	8
Preface	11
Introduction	12
Our Divine Nature	15
Sonship	39
Angels	65
Kingdom Generosity	85
Honor	101
The Advancing Kingdom	115
Prophetic Culture	129
Conclusion	147

Endorsements

Greater Chicago Church is living the core values in this book. I've watched them distill each one down and work it out. The result of actually wrestling with a cause and calling while leading a team of people committed to the vision is credibility. Ian Carroll and his team apply this book and invite people from around the world to join them. I'm excited to see what can happen when leaders work together on paradigms, principles, and relationships aligned with the Kingdom of heaven. I highly recommend *As It Is In Heaven*.

Danny Silk

Author of *Culture of Honor, Loving Our Kids On Purpose, Powerful & Free,* and *Keep Your Love On*

I am always happy to write endorsements of books on a subject dear to my heart, but I am even happier when I get to endorse a person and their book. This is the case with this book. I can endorse the book very easily because I know the man and have consistently been encouraged by him. I love real people who have real life experiences who use their lives to encourage others. Ian is one of these people. When it comes to culture you will, as Ian says, only really succeed in changing the culture around you when it has changed inside of you.

Ian is a man with an extraordinary set of life experiences who has never ceased to learn and desire to expand the boundaries of his life experience. This book is the fruit of that journey and the fruit of you reading this will be that there will be fruit in your life. It will be the kind of fruit that inspires you to believe that there is more and that you can be a part of bringing change to your environment. Fruit that says you should not be limited by your life experience, but know that it is the springboard for more. Ian's journey is anything but limited, yes it's practical and real, but it is also extraordinary and embraces the unseen and supernatural.

This is a book that will change you because it is written by a man who has embraced change and leads others into their change. His journey from patrolling streets to desiring that Chicago be a city changed by God will inspire and equip you.

I love this man, I love his vision and his heart and am honored to call him friend.

Paul Manwaring

Author of *Kisses from a Good God* and *What On Earth is Glory?*

Ian Carroll is a great thinker and powerful influencer. His book, *As It Is In Heaven* is an overflow of his contagious passion to see transformation happen in our lives, cities, and nations. This book will inspire you to believe it can and will happen. As Ian shares the core values he has established in the Greater Chicago ministry he leads, you will be equipped with the priorities and ways of thinking that will put you in the middle of what God is doing now on planet earth. Lastly, the chapter he writes on angels is worth the book alone. Well done, Ian.

Steve Backlund

Author of *Let's Just Laugh At That, Victorious Mindsets, Help! I'm a Pastor,* and *The Culture of Empowerment*

Preface

Everyone seems to want change, but no one really wants to change. Change gets people elected, it brings hope and fear, and our relationship with it is pretty complicated. I talk about change quite a bit. Change happens when we change what we believe, and our beliefs are changed when we start thinking differently about something. In the Bible, this is called repentance.

People who believe things they know to be untrue could be classified as mentally ill. Or as politicians. (Just kidding.) The problem with believing something to be true is it can be very difficult to start believing something different when you find out what you believed is not the actual truth. For most of us, it requires either an encounter with our promised future or some kind of crisis to change what we think. Most people reading this book are likely doing so because of the promises for your future.

Beliefs are changed over time by course-correcting our thinking. A useful tool I have found to change my beliefs is to make ongoing declarations about it. Something seems to shift inside me when I start hearing my own words agree with my destiny. I don't do it once and then stop. I do it continually—in prayer, when I walk, even when I play golf or work out. With the advent of Bluetooth headsets, people assume you are speaking on the phone and not deranged when they hear you talking to yourself! On my website_(www.icarroll.com) you have access to my daily declarations (#mydailydeclarations) which are free for you to use, download, and print for your reference and use.

This book started as a resource to help people who are new to Greater Chicago Church become familiar with who we are as a church. As interest grew, it morphed into what you hold in your hands. My prayers are that it will help transform and equip you into becoming all God intended you to be.

Introduction

If I had a dollar for every time I connect with a pastor or guest at our church who tells me they love what God is doing at Greater Chicago Church, I would be on my way to buying my dream Dodge Viper! People regularly experience the freedom in the place and the warmth of the people. The Presence of God is often thick—so thick that I frequently remark that if we had experienced this before 1994 when the Toronto Blessing happened, we would have thought full-on revival had hit us. People ask me how we do it, and pastors often tell me that they would love to have what we have.

They may initially think that what they are experiencing is a culture of honor or our prophetic culture and home in on one particular aspect of who we are. My wife, Rachel, recently said she feels that the experience people have when they come into our church home is the spirit of adoption. I think she is right. It is finding home, a place where you have been chosen and accepted and where you will change to become all you are called to be. God has given us the desire for a home. "Some wandered in desert places searching for a place to call home" (paraphrase of Psalm 107:4). Adoption itself is traumatic for the child. Even when an adoption has been wonderful, a child experiences a lot of adjustment. Some even go as far to say that adoption is similar to abduction for the child. Think about what it would be like, especially if the child is older. One day someone comes and takes you to a different home and you have to adjust, learn, and become part of a different family.

We experience the same thing. Many times, the freedom is a lot to grasp, the love can bring up many insecurities, and sonship can feel so risky. Those who have been looking for a home, a place where they are accepted and yet challenged to be transformed, will embrace this new family culture and grow into the person God has made them to be. We are in the business of raising sons and daughters in the atmosphere of heaven.

It wasn't always like this: we chose to change our church culture. Now there is a word every Christian loves—change. Change is easy; transitioning is difficult. It is not the change itself but the emotional connection with what is changing that defines a transition, and managing these transitions can be challenging. It is tough because people get scared, and they often aren't their best selves in those moments. It's also difficult because every change comes with loss. We lose what we have known and have become familiar with, and even if it is dysfunctional behavior that is changing, we can feel we are being tossed at sea, not knowing how to get to shore. We know we can't behave that way any more, but oftentimes we don't yet have the skills to behave in a "new" way.

Churches often start with their values and then build a future based on those. That isn't real change in my opinion, it is simply codifying what already exists. We started with fathers and mothers in the Kingdom—people who built something we loved. We explored their values, created a picture of our vision, and asked them, "What values do we need to get rid of and what values do we need to embrace to do what we want to do?" We got rid of some values and embraced others. Some people look at a church like Bethel in Redding, California and try to import every program they have, thinking it is the programs that make Bethel "successful." That is unwise. It is silly to look at a church, mimic everything they do, import all their programs, and think it will work elsewhere. That isn't transformation: it's wearing someone else's clothes. Without the work of discovering who you as a church are called to be, it is impossible to adapt another church's programs well. The process of change is like a mountaineering expedition. As with any expedition, there will be delays, setbacks, losses, injuries, exhilaration, disappointments, and days when you just want to go back and sleep in your own bed. But you will summit. You will reach the place you always intended to go if you don't quit, if you plan well, and if you enjoy every step you take. Always choose culture over programs.

This book is a description of the values and beliefs that currently define Greater Chicago Church. I describe our church like a cake, and people like our cake. Our values and beliefs are the ingredients of our cake, and sometimes people will say, "I don't really like or agree with this value," and I explain that it isn't a stir-fry, it's a cake. If you leave out an ingredient, you will produce something, but you won't get cake and you definitely won't get our cake. Sonship is one value people often try to negotiate into something else, and it's the same with honor. People often hear it, and they begin to try to change their definition of what I am saying so they never have to change. This is our cake. Enjoy it!!!

1

Our Divine Nature

Everyone seems to be speaking about identity, and frankly a lot of it is subpar. It is such a hot topic at the minute, championed by television personalities and preachers alike. Everyone needs that God-shaped hole in their beings filled with something, but to look at identity through a secular, humanistic lens will leave one still needing something to fill the void. We are born to be partakers of His nature through His promises. *"He has granted to us His precious and magnificent promises, so that by them you may become partakers of the divine nature"* (2 Peter 1:4).

The common secular humanistic approach is to believe "I'm not in need of change," whereas the true Christian realizes the need to be like Jesus (the very definition of holiness). Often though, both for the secularist and the Christian, the definition of holiness is rooted in an inferior view of who we are. It is as if God made us and has not been pleased with what He made, so we need to change to be the most unlike ourselves we can be. This results in striving and never feeling we are good enough. We think, "I will try to get away from being me rather than moving toward becoming fully me." The goal, however, is to be transformed *into* something rather than transformed *away* from something. The two pits on either side of the road of knowing who God made us to be are (1) low self-worth, which results in trying to change to please others, and (2) knowing we are amazing, which results in us refusing the need for transformation because we were born okay the first time.

Based on what others have told us about God, we have created an image of God. We start to become like the image of God that we have created. If God is judgmental in your image of Him, you will be judgmental. You become like the God you believe in. You will imitate the God you believe in and believe that is what being Holy is. You become what you behold.

As a young Christian (I think I had been saved for ten days at the time), I went door to door asking people to complete a survey. At the time, I thought it was a real survey and was shocked when my pastor simply discarded the survey results I had so diligently collected. Teams of two would go from house to house in my neighborhood, asking whoever answered the door if they would be willing to complete a survey. We asked some standard questions and then asked the questions that really mattered: "Do you believe in God?" "Do you go to church?" "Would you call yourself a Christian?" At this point, if they answered yes, we would ask, "How long have you been a Christian?" If they told us the age at which they got saved at, we would ask them to pray for us as we evangelized door to door. If they answered, "All my life," we would begin the process of convincing them they needed to make a personal decision for Jesus and not rely on their parents or some sacrament to get them to heaven.

Of course if someone answered that he was not a Christian, we would ask "Why not?" and then begin trying to convince them of their need to be saved. For us, and I would argue the vast majority of the Evangelical Church, convincing people of their need to be saved was an attempt to convince people that though they are worthless, God, in His Mercy, would gladly accept them because He loves them despite the fact they are utterly worthless. We would have to convince them of their worthlessness to be effective. Heck, it was how I got saved!

Recently I have been aware of how some of that early teaching still affects me. I was meditating on the scripture that says Jesus intercedes for us (Romans 8:34). In the old mindset, I have an image of a nice Jesus pleading with an angry Father God to have mercy on me. Jesus, in this picture, is more kind than the Father. This is nonsense, because Jesus is the perfect representation of the Father, and if you have seen Him, you have seen the Father. Nonetheless, if I have a warped image of God and how He sees me, I find myself relating to either a merciful, pleading Jesus or an angry Father. I am born to be *like* God (no—I am not born to *be* God), I am called to become like Jesus, I was created in His image, and I have a God-given bent to be like Him—but I will re-present the image of the God I have formed in my mind. I will become what I behold.

Identity theft

I have always been told that man's first sin was pride. Satan appeared and offered Eve the temptation of being like God. He told her that God did not want her to eat from the second tree because He knew that when she did, her eyes would be opened and she would be like God.

There can be an accusation about God in this—that God was afraid of Adam and Eve knowing they were powerful and could understand good and evil. There seemed to be the planting of a seed in fertile ground. I wonder if Adam and Eve had not already been doubting, wondering, and believing things about God at that point. Seldom does the devil win with a single temptation if there is not already some fertile soil to plant in. Satan started by misrepresenting God's command by asking, "Has not God said to not eat from any tree?" (Genesis 3:1) and went on to tell Eve that she would not die by eating from the forbidden tree. He used accusation, misrepresentation, and lies. All of these tools remain in the toolbox of the devil. There was also an attempt to divide the man and the woman. Eve was not present when God commanded Adam to not eat from the second tree. Satan was introducing division between the man and the woman; he was introducing mistrust in their relationship, and mistrust about power, authority, and submission.

So what was the accusation? The misrepresentation? The lie? The real thing going on was that the devil fed something that I suspect was already festering. Adam and Eve likely had an underlying doubt that they were actually made in the image of God and were really like God. God is not afraid of us knowing that we are made in His image; in fact His heart breaks when we consider ourselves as less than He has made us. To say that God fears our knowing that we are powerful is reducing God to insecurity. He is totally secure in who He is and who He has called us to be. We hold the mandate to be fruitful and multiply, to fill the earth and subdue it, and to rule—a mandate given to us by God Himself.

Satan was cast from heaven to earth because he wanted to be like God. God decided that to defeat Satan on earth, He would create a race that was like God. The very thing that Satan wanted was given to another, and he is the one who is fearful of our knowing who we are. He is the one who is jealous and despises that God chose us and has plans to prosper us, to give us a future and a hope (Jeremiah 29:11), whereas Satan only has a lake of fire for a destiny.

My belief is that pastors and teachers have cooperated more with Satan, when it comes to our identity, than with God. All of us are, every single human being is—created in the image of God. We know that when God said "Let us make him in our likeness" (Genesis 1:27), it does not mean we serve a God with arms and legs. It means that at our core, we look like the Trinity. It takes man and woman to represent God. God delights in opposites, heaven and earth, land and sea, darkness and light, male and female. It is this diversity that attracts fruitfulness and abundance.

Our identity has been stolen by the devil, and much of the Church has cooperated with him. To help people feel their worthlessness, we berate them as sinners. When they don't believe they are sinners, we define sin for them. For those who respond, we bring them into church families that are often afraid when people start thinking "too much" of themselves. So we use Scripture to keep them down and convince them they are privileged to even be in church and should not get too high and mighty. We appoint pastors who are not really pastors, but people with a gift of mercy or service. These false pastors, often self-appointed and self-anointed, keep people stuck in the belief that they are unworthy and really need the rescue of those who minister.

The Church has been hurt more by false pastors than false prophets and false apostles. These false pastors enjoy being needed and being the top of the ministry food chain. Sound too harsh? I assure you I have watered this down. We have tolerated people being held down and stuck in unhealthy places under the guise of "pastoring." True pastoring releases everyone into their true identity and calls them into being all they were created to be. The disciples became arrogant and full of their own identities to the extent that they knew they could call down fire from heaven, and they were even bold enough to ask to sit at the right hand of Jesus. People in the company of Jesus start to feel better about themselves and believe they have been created for something significant. People in the hands of false pastors never get over their own unworthiness and sense of failure and end up settling to not rule, to not be fruitful, and to not have authority.

I believe that after salvation, the most important thing we need as children of God is to feel good about who we are—to have a healthy dose of self-worth. As with any truth, it can manifest in an immature way. As adolescents, we think we can drive better than anyone else and think we know more about most things than anyone else, especially our parents and teachers. We do not parent our immature children in a way that makes them feel worthless (at least I hope we don't). We continue to encourage them to listen, to be teachable, and to understand that they have not arrived but are in fact on a journey. It is the same with the immature adolescents who discover they are born to be amazing. They can say screwy things and behave in ways that seem inappropriate, but our response should not be to change who God says they are. It should be to get them to look at how amazing Jesus is. No matter how amazing I think I am, one look at Him makes me pale by comparison.

What God Says About Us

Throughout all translations of the Bible, Hebrews 2:9 states that Jesus was made a little lower than the angels, a quote likely taken from the Greek version of the Old Testament rather than directly from the Hebrew text. Hebrews 2:9 is a quote from Psalm 8:5, where it is translated in all but one major translation as "being made a little lower than God." Man has been made a little lower than God. The Hebrew word is *Elohim*, which is never translated as angels anywhere else. It is one of the first words used in the Bible: "In the beginning God [Elohim] created ..." (Genesis 1:1). This word is translated as God 2,239 times. Could it be that some translators of Scripture saw what this actually meant and decided it was too scandalous to be true? That would surely place angels and demons beneath us on the created beings hierarchy of authority and power. Yet God made us in His image and crowned us with glory and power.

When the Godhead, the Elohim, gathered in Genesis and made a decision that the earth was good, that everything He had created was good, He decided to make man in "our image." That is the same word that is used when Adam had a son in Genesis 5 and called him Seth. The son was the image of the father. In the same way, we are the image of our Father. The family resemblance is remarkable! You have to believe that Cain, Abel, and Seth looked just like their mother and father. There were no grandparents and no diluted DNA, but simply the DNA of their mother and father. They were copies of their parents. We too are copies of our Father. Of course, sin got in the way, but Jesus dealt with that once and for all on the cross. The second Adam, Jesus, was greater than the first and destroyed sin and restored us to be children of God. Our sins were removed and our very sin nature was destroyed. Adam managed to sin without a sin nature, and so can we even though our old nature has been destroyed. But the issue is no longer about sin; the issue is about living as we should live as images of our Father. It's not trying to get away from sin, but rather it is moving toward our heavenly identities.

Who Do You Say That You Are?

Proverbs 18:21 tells us that death and life are in the power of the tongue. Who we say we are is really important. The truth that "out of the overflow of the mouth, the heart speaks" tells me that it isn't just the words we say that are important but the heart of what we believe.

I believe that 99.9% of spiritual warfare is engaged in the space between our ears! The battle most of us fight is the warfare between lies and truth. The problem with lies is that they seem so plausible. They comfort us, give us reasons to sin, and in them we find ways for our lives and the advancement of the Kingdom to be out of whack with Scripture. If I don't see people healed, then it must be God's fault, or as we sometimes put it, not His will. This is a ridiculous lie.

We are in a war for our minds. We simply must believe what God says, not what our parents, our teachers, and our preachers have told us, and certainly not the bullies and detractors who have told us we will not amount to anything. This warfare is for a mind renewed on earth as it will be in heaven.

Changing our minds and hearts starts with understanding the right things about who God says we are. Once we have the truth, we can start adjusting our beliefs through declarations.

Listen to what you really believe about yourself. Reflect on who you say you are every day. Do you say you are not enough, your education is not enough, your looks are not enough, and your job is not enough? Do you believe that you don't deserve kindness? Do you, when you are alone and the lights are out, believe that you are unlovable and will be justifiably rejected all your days? Simple statements like "I am stupid" are the overflow of what is going on in your heart—what you truly believe about yourself.

I don't want to get into the superstitious nonsense that is out there in some circles that you should not declare anything negative about yourself. The truth is that there are times when I have been stupid! It's good to admit that, deal with it, and move on, but it will never become how I define myself. The difference is that I don't actually believe I am stupid, so it comes with no weight. But if I say something negative that I really do believe in my heart, it is a declaration with faith attached. That is dangerous.

So how do I change my beliefs? Understand the truth, identify the lies, and make a decision that you want to and *will* believe differently. This is your battle, not someone else's, and not even God's though He will fight it with you. Surround yourself with people who will see who you are, see who God has called you to be, and start declaring things that align with your identity. This is one of the reasons I love my church family. They are the most encouraging people on the earth. It is why people on their own don't do well. You need to belong to a covenant family that will encourage the hell out of you. I am a blood-bought child of the Most High God. I walk in favor and great blessing. I have the mind of Christ, the heart of the Father, and the power of the Holy Spirit living in me. Goodness and abundance chase after me every day. I am called to equip the saints to minister and to win cities for the King. These are some of my declarations that I really believe and that are part of my daily devotional life.

But wait, you may be wondering, "You spend time declaring stuff over yourself as part of your devotions? Isn't that taking the focus off God?" The best thing each of us can do in prayer is focus on God, but we must also learn to encourage ourselves in the Lord. I remember a wise man once said that if he spent 15 minutes in prayer, he would pray for himself for 14 minutes and others for the remaining minute. Why? Because the best he could do was to be all God had called him to be as he healed the sick, delivered people from demons, and set captives free. Get your identity muscle in shape and you will outlast the most tiresome of days, you will do what you are called to do, and be who you were created to be.

Get yourself a prophetic identity. Get your identity from heaven's perspective, and start believing in who He says you are. I don't believe in generational curses, I do believe there are scripts handed down to us from our parents, grandparents, etc. These scripts are often complete lies. They tell us people like us will never be rich, will never amount to anything, and the best we can hope for is to have a house, two kids, and an occasional vacation. They tell us we get less than we work for and that the best days are over. Yet Jesus tells us that He came to give us an abundant life and freedom. Abundance and freedom are always, always, always issues of the heart and mind, not issues of your bank account and right to vote.

The Lie of Humility

It is fair to say that I have not always made it easy to be part of Greater Chicago Church. I like change and the Holy Spirit leads me. If you know anything about the person of the Holy Spirit, you will know that He operates like the wind: you don't know where He is going or coming from. You just need to follow. He is by His very nature creative, loves to explore new things, and His business is change. He changes us, He changes nations, and we must learn to change. All increase will involve change, and He loves to bring increase!

One time, I had a wonderful member of our church meet with me to tell me he was leaving. This was a loss for us as a church as he was a stable, mature influence in our church. He was the stereotype of a good Christian man in every way you could imagine. He was a successful, wealthy, well-balanced man with decades of giving and serving under his belt and he exuded modesty and humility. He was and is a great guy. At our meeting, he told me that what he wanted from a church was to look up after he had closed his eyes for prayer and see a room filled with people who look just like him. I don't know if he meant white, successful professionals, but something in me laughed and thought "You will never find that with us." Here was a godly man in outward—and I am sure many inward—ways, who would be applauded in many churches, and I was actually glad he was leaving. When people heard he was leaving, they would always make mention of his humility and I would struggle to agree.

There has been a facade of humility in the church for a long time. Humility, it seems, means never getting angry (sorry Jesus, You are out, You should not have fashioned a whip), always being steady and slow to change (sorry Holy Spirit, it seems You are out, all this wind blowing where it wants is too flaky), and never being undignified (sorry Father, but the image of the father in the story of the prodigal hitching his clothes into his drawers and running toward his son is not appropriate). Somehow when Creflo Dollar asks for donations to buy a plane it's a scandal: but when Bill Hybels uses Willow Creek's plane it's okay. The church image of humility is largely white, stoic, and proper. It is largely a denial of identity.

How should I deal with scriptures that tell me to let my light shine before men, such as Matthew 5:16? Not Jesus' light, my light. And not before God for an audience of one, but before men? Then it goes on to say that they would see my good works—my good works, not God's—and as a result glorify the Father in heaven. Is it possible that the Church is stalled because we are afraid of powerful people, and feel that in order to be successful pastors, we must have no one more powerful than we are?

Let me be clear. I lead and ask people to follow me. Some follow, some follow for a while, and some don't follow. I am the leader, called to be an apostle not because I am the most educated, the most gifted, the most anointed, the most prophetic, the best dancer, or the most handsome. I am the leader, the apostle, because that is who God has called me to be and it annoys people who either are or who think they are more gifted, anointed, or handsome than I am. In my opinion, it is this manifestation of false humility that keeps the powerful people in society outside the Church. Many identify as being spiritual, but in the Church they discover leaders who need to keep people down and keep them from being more powerful, more famous, more wealthy, and more influential than the pastor in charge. The promotion of this brand of false humility has a root of insecurity at its core.

True humility is rooted in security. I am secure in who God says I am and what I am called to do. This hasn't always been the case. In fact I have spent much of my time hiding from titles, positions, and influence, being afraid of the white, stable millionaires. Like Jonah, I suspect we run and hide from our assignments because we are afraid of what others may say. Jonah was given a call to ask Israel's enemies to repent and to tell them they would not be judged. Can you imagine the accusations that would bring from his kinsmen?

We have a system in the Church that is broken. We appoint pastors and leaders based on their qualifications or perhaps their "niceness." The moment someone more qualified or nice comes along, then a threat to my security has just entered the room. So I teach on denying yourself. After all, it's in the Bible right?

Wrong. I would suggest that denying yourself is different from denying who God made you to be. Denying your gifts and call is like telling God His gifts are not good enough or that He got it wrong by choosing you. Denying yourself is about denying your propensity for mediocrity. Jonah's "cross to bear" was to be a prophet to an entire nation, causing national repentance and the salvation of a city. Yet most of us think that if Jonah were really following after God, God's will would be to have him act like a slave and be on that ship to nowhere or to lie in the belly of the whale. Denying yourself is to deny living in the belly of a whale, accepting whatever will be will be. Jonah's "vain idol" was not becoming a great man in the eyes of a nation; it was forsaking being a great man in the eyes of a nation. The NIV translates Jonah 2:8 as "Those who cling to worthless idols forfeit the grace that could be theirs." Your God-given identity is not a worthless idol. What parent would delight in their children seeing their identities, gifts, and calls as a piece of dung? I will reiterate; you are a child of God, made in His image. You are precious in His sight, and He has uniquely gifted and called you for a purpose. None of that is a worthless idol. Running away from it because you feel less than others, you are the wrong color, the wrong gender, not educated enough, or simply not the best person to do it in your eyes—these are all worthless idols, and coming under the influence of these lies will forfeit the grace of God that He uses to propel you toward your destiny.

We have made an idol of the white, middle-aged man who is steady and safe and whose investment may mean he has a net worth of millions, but he will keep it all under wraps under the guise of humility. This has got to change. The world is not groaning for the return of Jesus. It is groaning for the manifestation of a people who know they are sons and daughters of a King and who do not lord it over people, but at the same time are not afraid of being as amazing as their Father desires, as full as His Son paid for, and as free as His Spirit empowers them.

Women

"I do not permit a woman to teach or to have authority over a man; she must be silent" (1 Timothy 2:12).

Biblical scholars have noted that the word translated as "to have authority" (which in Greek is the word *authentein*) has a forceful and extremely negative connotation. It implies a more specific meaning than "to have authority over" and can be translated "to dominate," "to usurp," or "to take control." Often when this word was used in ancient Greek literature, it was associated with violence or even murder. A clearer picture of what Paul told Timothy is that Paul doesn't allow a woman to violently steal authority. But are we to think that Paul would allow a man to violently steal authority just because he is a man? Obviously, the issue was not gender. In reference to this specific problem, Paul was instructing Timothy not to allow these women who were trying to take control and usurp authority to speak or have influence. It was a church management issue, not a gender issue.

In Paul's letter to Titus, Paul addressed a similar problem. In this case, it was men who were causing the problem: *"For there are many rebellious men, empty talkers and deceivers, especially those of the circumcision, who must be silenced because they are upsetting whole families, teaching things they should not teach for the sake of sordid gain"* (Titus 1:10–11). The fact that this verse has never been used to tell all men everywhere that they must be silent and cannot teach is indicative of the one-sided and male-dominated approach that the Church has taken toward women.

At the start of creation, male and female were created in the likeness—the kind—of God. If we diminish the role of women, we will reduce our view of God. For fruitfulness to happen, the equal and real presence of male and female must be actualized, not hypothesized. I don't want to get all weird, but to be fruitful, it takes a man and a woman to be together. No one has gotten someone pregnant from sexting! This is not a complementary role but an equal partnership in the act of fruitfulness. The need for opposites is clear in creation: light and dark, sea and land, earth and sky. For the church to be truly fruitful, for humankind to rule, we must have both men and women released into all they are called to be.

In the garden, the devil came to Eve not because she was the weaker party, but because she was as powerful as the man. Satan hates women. It is why some of the earth's greatest atrocities are perpetrated on women. Abortion, sex trafficking, China's one child rule, inequality throughout every society—all victimize women more than men and often in unspeakable ways. Even the Church has told women who have suffered at the hands of abusive husbands that their job is to submit and be quiet. They are told it's their God-given place as wives to submit to the fists of the one who abuses them because that is God's way. This is preposterous and demonic. If a wife is being abused by her husband, he has broken his covenant to lay down his life for her and love her, and she should get out of there as fast as possible. The scripture commanding wives to submit to their husbands is often taken out of context. The context is that we submit to each other out of reverence for Christ. Submission is a vital element in the life of every believer, but it is not solely the responsibility of wives. I would argue that it is the posture of every son and daughter to be in submission and to lay down our lives for the sake of another, but a Church led by men for centuries in a world system that has decided to keep women "less than" has kept women back—and the Kingdom has suffered.

If "a man is the head of a woman" in 1 Corinthians 11:3 means that he is her boss, then how do we explain God being the head of Christ? Is Christ not co-equal with God? Did He not consider Himself equal with God but just didn't use that equality for His life here on earth? We have such a hierarchical mindset around this notion of headship that has betrayed women and held the church back.

In Israel prior to King David, a woman ruled the nation. Her name was Deborah. God has no issue with women ruling and no issue with men submitting to women. In Judges 4, Barak submitted to Deborah. Deborah even told him he would not have the honor, as the Lord was about to deliver the enemy into the hands of a woman. Still Barak fought and overcame. The church needs men like Barak—men who will submit to and serve women with no reserve and it needs women like Deborah—women who are not afraid of leading and are ready to take their place as apostles, prophets, pastors, teachers, and evangelists, and not just in kids church. The church needs to support women CEOs, women entrepreneurs, women politicians, and also women who choose to raise kids for whatever season they decide.

After the events of Genesis 3, God placed a curse upon the serpent, a curse upon the woman, and a curse upon the ground that Adam would be tending. The curse that was placed upon the woman is the curse that caused the gender war. What was the curse upon the woman? *"To the woman He said, 'I will greatly increase your pains in childbearing; with pain you will give birth to children. Your desire will be for your husband, and he will rule over you'"* (Genesis 3:16).

The key is in the word "desire," translated from the Hebrew *tesuqah*, which occurs only three times in the Old Testament. It is best understood through its usage in Genesis 4:7, which shows another side—that of a desire to overcome or defeat another: "[Sin's] desire is for you, but you should rule over it." God is saying that a woman's desire will be to gain the upper hand over her husband, but because she is physically weaker, her husband will put her down by force, if need be. The curse was essentially that women would lose the battle of the sexes. That was the curse for sinning, but thankfully there was a solution. There was One who would come and break all curses. What the first Adam did, the second Adam would undo through His death and resurrection. God released the curses for rebellion, including the subjugation of woman.

Adam named his wife. Until this point in the story (see Genesis 1–3:19), his wife was only referred to as the woman, but now Adam gives her a name and the woman becomes Eve. This may seem small and insignificant, but if we consider that Adam and the woman had walked as equals before the curse, this is actually a profound detail.

Previously, in Genesis 1:28, Adam and Eve had been given dominion to rule over all the animals, birds, and fish; but Adam did not rule over woman until the curse occurred. When the woman received the curse of subjugation, Adam named her in the same manner that he had named all the animals of the garden (see Genesis 2:19–20). By naming the woman, Adam took dominion over Eve in the same way that he took dominion over the animals. And so the curse was applied and enacted. God called this a curse because He never desired for them to be unequal. It was not God's intention but rather a result of sin. Humanity is made in the image of God, male and female together. Taking one half out and calling it "complementary" is akin to making women "less than" and diminishing our God-given identity. Jesus came and destroyed all barriers. There is no longer Jew and Greek, male or female. Jesus was born of a woman. The first person to touch Jesus was His mother, Mary, a pure young woman who was esteemed more than any other woman. The first person to touch the resurrected Jesus was Mary Magdalene, a woman with a less than pure life and history but whom Jesus had made clean. Jesus was a friend of women—scandalous in His day.

There is no position in the church that women are to be excluded from. To say otherwise is misguided at best and prejudiced at worst.

Society's Biggest Question

For ages people have asked the questions: "What are we here for?" and "What is this all about?" How has the church answered? Many times by telling people that their chief aim is to glorify God: images of worship services with dull organ music or people stuck in one of the many renewals come to mind. Nowadays, most of us have no idea what it actually means to glorify God and enjoy Him forever.

In Psalm 8, God answers the question for us. We

have been crowned to rule and have all things under our feet. Our purpose on earth is to rule. Yet we have reduced humanity's purpose to getting their sins forgiven.

Don't get me wrong—we needed our sins forgiven. All of us must submit to Jesus as our Lord and Savior. We must confess our sins and accept His forgiveness. Any reliance on our own works to make the cut is pure self-righteousness and not faith-righteousness. We enter something completely new once we have decided to follow Jesus, but this moment of salvation, being born again, is the start of something. Many get stuck on the moment of birth rather than the life that follows. I think this has been around for centuries. Even the Apostles Creed leaves out most of the four Gospel accounts of Jesus' life. The Gospels are not a Passion narrative, finally getting to the main point. The reason we are stuck is that we believe we are worthless, but God saves us, so one day we will die and go to be with Him. Just like the Apostles Creed celebrates the birth and death and resurrection of Jesus but leaves out His life and ministry, so we celebrate our new birth and anticipate being with Him but neglect our reason to be here on earth.

We are born again to rule, but that requires authority and power. We do not receive authority and power because of anything we do—again that would be self-righteousness—but we receive it because of what Jesus did for us and what He gave us. The notion that I lose my authority and power because I sin is erroneous. It is not based on my works at all. This is why powerful men and women who have fantastic success in healing and miracles can be found sinning on the side. Their authority and power is not dependent on their behavior.

Behavior matters but is not necessary to access a gift. Jesus did away with sin being the block to us taking our place and doing what we were put on earth to do, but behavior matters. It matters for relationships and for happiness. Behavior matters because God wants us to have an abundant life, not a life overshadowed by dark secrets and broken relationships. It matters because it helps us be intimate with each other and with God, and it matters because sinning erodes your self-worth. I can't imagine anyone with low self-worth speaking to a mountain and casting it into the sea.

In my time as a human being and as a church leader, I have found that people are afraid of confessing their sins, often until they are discovered or found out. Shame and humiliation are poor motivations for real change, even the change needed to simply embrace the finished work of the cross. We ask people to confess to an angry God and even angrier church leaders. We each know everything that is wrong about us, and the only solution to that can be found in Christ. But if we believe that He will punish us, then the very One we must go to becomes the last One we will go to. We are ashamed of going time and again for the same thing or things and avoid going to Him all together. The person we should talk to is Jesus, and to do that we must know that He does not hold our sins against us, and will not repay us as our sins deserve. If you read that in any context other than the spaciousness between east and west, you missed the point. When He doesn't repay us as our sins deserve, it doesn't mean we get forgiven but scowled at or that we get forgiven and still need to face the consequences; it means that as far as God is concerned, the sin never happened. One thing God cannot do is remember your sins because He has chosen to remember them no more.

When I became a Christian at 15 years old, I doubted my salvation. I probably asked Jesus to save me dozens of times in those first few months. I feared I had backslid if I even missed a church meeting or didn't pray for a day. Those around me pointed to scriptures that assured me of my salvation and once I believed these Scriptures, once I placed my faith on the truth of knowing I was saved, I never doubted that I was going to heaven. That is probably familiar to most of us. It was a decision, followed by doubt, followed by memorizing Scripture and believing it to be true. But what about the rest of Scripture? What about the piece that promises all the benefits of salvation—benefits that help us with our God-mandated purpose here on earth?

Bless the Lord, O my soul,

And all that is within me, bless His holy name.

Bless the Lord, O my soul,

And forget none of His benefits;

Who pardons all your iniquities,

Who heals all your diseases;

Who redeems your life from the pit,

Who crowns you with lovingkindness and compassion;

Who satisfies your years with good things,

So that your youth is renewed like the eagle (Psalm 103: 1–5).

Can we start memorizing scriptures like this one and take it as truth, just as we did for our salvation? Can we start actually believing that we minister in the Name that is above all Names? We minister in the name of Jesus, who was given all authority in heaven and then commanded us, as ones under that authority and carrying that authority, to go and make disciples of nations? What would it look like if we put as much effort into believing these scriptures as we did into our salvation experience?

I used to hear the statement "What we believe about something is more important than the something" as a defeat. I wanted the "something" to change so my belief about it was not important. I have grown up a little since then. When it comes to our identities, what we believe—and I mean really believe—about who we are is crucial. Prosperity, healing, authority, and favor will be stalled if we believe we are worms and are apathetic about ruling on this earth as God intended us to do. Changing our mindsets is pretty straightforward, but we must want them changed. Many of us develop secondary benefits from patterns of needing to be rescued, being victims, and being helpless to do anything that will change us. In order to protect what little self-worth we have, we build defenses around our mental constructs. It seems we couldn't bear to have been wrong for the last 30 years as that would shatter our limited self-worth altogether, so we cling to old mindsets and old ways of thinking. The belief that "If only I had different parents, then I would be able to believe" is unacceptable. You are a new creation. God deals with us from the present to the future and can heal our past.

Some hunt for demons to blame and cast out, or supposed spirits of lust, instead of personally taking responsibility for who they are now and who they are called to be. Demons have access largely through what we believe—the lies we have been fed. Replacing these lies with truth will guarantee that any demonic hold in our lives will be lost forever. If the lies are not replaced with truth, that old thing will come back with some friends because it will know that you have not cleaned your house! (Matthew 12:45). Most of us are not changed by reacting to a negative; we are changed when we realize the perfection of Jesus already lives inside of us, and our job is to bring what is present into our reality. You are a child of God, created in His image. For God to stop loving you would mean He would have to stop loving Jesus because you are in Christ and Christ is in you.

Every thought you have produces something. There is no such thing as an impotent thought. Your thoughts produce good fruit or bad fruit. When you think about something, the cutting edge of neuroscience tells us it either increases our health or decreases our health. We are designed to live in truth. This truth that you are God's image, created in His likeness, will shape your destiny.

"But I still sin," you may say. Adam and Eve sinned without having a sin nature, and so can you. But your identity is not as a sinner; your identity is as a saint. Sin will only be conquered when you destroy the fortresses of your mind that are built around a fake identity (who the accuser says you are) and replace it with who God says you are.

The first step to learning to rule is to learn to rule over your own life. Be in charge: be the one who is seeking first the Kingdom instead of waiting for some event to happen that will propel you into your destiny. The Kingdom is a realm where all the promises of God are yes in Jesus and we get to place our amen onto that Divine yes! Amen means "may it be fulfilled." Start putting words to your identity. Start putting words to your destiny. Add your voice to the promises of God and speak your "Amen." He has promised, and now we get to be vocal about who He has said we are and what he has called us to do. Stir up the identity that is inside you.

When Jesus was tempted in the wilderness, He did not have images of naked women paraded in front of Him. He did not have fast, fancy chariots or whatever people coveted in those days. Satan addressed his identity: "If you are the Son of God ..." Satan's tactics have not changed since the Garden of Eden. He tried and will try to make all of us feel less than who God has made us to be. Submit yourself to God's identity of you, and resist the Devil and he will flee.

2

Sonship

We are servants of God. Let me first affirm this truth. There are times in all our lives when to know the truth of this and grow in what it means for us is incredibly important.

We are also, collectively, the Bride of Christ. This romance with Jesus has produced some of the most intimate worship from my heart and draws me toward Him. It is important to know these principles do not change. For some who are in the middle of learning to serve or to be wooed, talking about sonship can seem like the wrong focus.

The people who walk in darkness

Will see a great light;

Those who live in a dark land,

The light will shine on them.

You shall multiply the nation,

You shall increase their gladness;

They will be glad in Your presence

As with the gladness of harvest,

As men rejoice when they divide the spoil.

For You shall break the yoke of their burden and the staff on their shoulders,

The rod of their oppressor, as at the battle of Midian.

For every boot of the booted warrior in the battle tumult,

And cloak rolled in blood, will be for burning, fuel for the fire.

For a child will be born to us, a son will be given to us;

And the government will rest on His shoulders;

And His name will be called Wonderful Counselor, Mighty God,

Eternal Father, Prince of Peace.

There will be no end to the increase of His government or of peace,

On the throne of David and over his kingdom,

To establish it and to uphold it with justice and righteousness

From then on and forevermore.

The zeal of the Lord of hosts will accomplish this (Isaiah 9:2–7).

This prophetic eschatological passage speaks of the coming of a King who will rule and reign on heaven and on earth. A child is born and a son given, and I suggest that the government of heaven on earth rests on sons and daughters. There is a connection between the rule or dominion of God on earth and us showing up as sons or daughters. When I think of some of my heroes of modern times (Bill Johnson and John and Carol Arnott to name three), I am struck that they show up in their lives and leadership as sons and daughters, not as fathers and mothers. Many, including me, have given them the place of fathers and mothers, but they manifest this quality of sonship which makes them easy to follow.

When I start talking about becoming a son, many people think immediately of the abuses, the serious abuses, of previous movements in the church, particularly the discipleship movement in the 70s and 80s. They hear me say that I want a subservient people waiting to mow my lawn and roof my house when I speak of sonship. Let me ask you a question: Is Jesus less than the Father? No. That would be nonsense and heretical. Sonship is not about hierarchy or authority; it's about how we as individuals manifest or show up in our own lives. The culture of heaven is not authority or even power: it is family. Not the "2.2 kids, a minivan, and a dog" family, but family relationships done well. Sonship is not a loss; it's not a taking away of your freedom, destiny, and will. It is not a theft of your greatness. In this Kingdom, those who want to be first must be last. Those who want to be greatest must be the least.

On my first visit to Bethel in Redding, California, I was wrecked. As a Vineyard pastor, I had seen it, done it, and bought the T-shirt. While waiting in line to register (it was such a long line that it took hours), I stood beside a woman and her 13-year-old daughter. This mother proceeded to tell everyone that she was Catholic and only had a few months to live, but God told her to come to this conference where she would be healed. I stood beside her, full of the faith of a different kingdom, and thought, "You silly woman. It is people like me that will have to deal with your daughter and the disappointment over this. The Kingdom is largely not-yet, so please don't build false hope and expectation into your daughter." A few nights later, this woman was healed. I later learned that she had an all-clear report from her doctor—and that on the way home, her daughter led a man to Jesus at the airport. This was pretty impressive, but it was not what struck me the most. It certainly brought back to life that deep desire for the miraculous, but I knew this thing called Bethel was more than miracles; it was family.

On the last evening, I took my seat and a feather fell from seemingly nowhere. One person got up to grab it. What appeared to be a Bethel member told the apparent visitor not to fuss because these things happen all the time. Shortly thereafter, an older man in his 70s sat in front of me and began introducing his son to the Bethel community. His son looked like he was experiencing cold turkey from drugs or alcohol and looked rough. His clothes were old but clean and had seen much better days, but his father paraded his awkward son in front of everyone as if the son were a Prince. After worship came the obligatory time to greet your neighbor. This is a component of worship services that, as an introvert, I dread. I stood up and the aforementioned father turned around and hugged me. I started the hug, and as a good pastor, I did the tap on the back after a few seconds to indicate I was done. But this older man was not done. He kept hugging me, and at that moment I broke. I wept on his shoulder for what seemed like an eternity. The thing I remember was that he never broke the hug. This man, probably eight inches shorter than I am and half my weight, held on to me like I meant everything to him. He was smiling, and I wept like a baby. Everyone else had sat down, and here I was, weeping uncontrollably on the shoulders of a stranger.

My earthly father died when I was 11 years old and I never got to say goodbye. I never heard the words that he was proud of me, and I don't remember him ever telling me that he loved me. This wound of losing my father has haunted me most of my days, and in the moment of worship and greeting at Bethel, I was held by a father who wanted to hold me.

My take-away that week was sonship. The only book I bought from the bookstore was *Spiritual Slavery to Spiritual Sonship* by Jack Frost. Jack had spoken at our church once, and what he said had gone in one ear and out the other. I had heard him speak at Toronto Airport Christian Fellowship, now Catch The Fire Toronto, and found him engaging but not earth shattering. His message of a loving, heavenly Father was great, but this book's of sonship gripped me. Something connected and I realized the path to a life in the Kingdom, the seeking first of the Kingdom, could only be walked by those who have a spirit of adoption rather than an orphan spirit. My realization would never have happened had it not been for an old man, proud of his wounded son, who did not let go of me.

Nine months later, I was the interim senior pastor of our church. Our senior pastor had resigned, and one of the other associate pastors and myself were tasked with navigating the church through a time of transition. I should point out that there was no sin, and the senior pastor resigned at the request of the leadership of the church, a leadership that included me. After he resigned, I decided to take the staff and church board to attend a Supernatural Strategic Planning session held at Bethel that was led by the leader of Global Legacy at Bethel church, Redding, Paul Manwaring. We went with the hope of finding out where we would go from here. It became apparent during the week that the main thing we needed to do was to appoint a senior pastor. Paul spent some time with each group that came, and during his time with us he made it clear that we needed a leader. Only Paul didn't use the word "leader"; he used the word "father." He asked everyone around our table if I was the father of the house. They all said yes. I can remember being terrified. I struggled with saying I wanted to do it because it felt tasteless to ask for someone's resignation and then end up replacing them. I knew the accusations that would arise, and I knew I would be rejected by some of our congregation. But once I decide something, I act on it. We left that week with the knowledge that I was to father our church.

Family—it is all about family. But not the western nuclear family. It is about fathers and mother, sons and daughters, running together, doing life together, and learning to never give up on relationships.

If we emphasize creating fathers and mothers, we step into some dangerous territory. If, like some Christian version of Darth Vader, I say that I am your father, what I am actually doing is assuming a role in your life that you may or may not have given me. It is a form of control. If I give someone the place of being a father or mother in my life, then that is totally different. It means I can manage my responses toward them. When I am disappointed by them, I get to manage those feelings. When I need something from them, I can ask. When I need correction, I decide whether I will listen or not. Sonship places the responsibility on the son or daughter, not the father or mother. Of course we need good fathers and mothers, but the best ones are those who have already learned to be sons and daughters. We get good fathers and mothers by raising sons and daughters.

I was radically impacted in 1994 by what is known as the "Toronto Blessing," or, as the leader of the church where it all started John Arnott calls it, "The Father's Blessing." The message that shook me and many in the Church was that the Father loves us. My horizontal view of fathering was pretty messed up, and I had projected that horizontal dysfunction onto my vertical view of our heavenly Father. I had believed and been taught that the Father was the stern, angry, judgmental part of the Godhead, Jesus was the good guy, and the Holy Spirit was a little flaky. The revelation from John and Carol that the Father loves us rocked my world and continues to influence me to this day. I couldn't care less about the shaking, roaring, and trance-like states that were happening in Toronto (I have done them all). What I cared about most was that the love of the Father had gripped me. I was not afraid of a stern God but loved by via the Father's embrace. I am indebted to John and Carol, have the privilege of knowing them and they are the real deal.

Despite such a phenomenal message, it did not always produce sons and daughters outside of Catch The Fire (CTF). It is vitally important to know who God the Father is, but that alone does not teach us how to manage ourselves, especially in relationship with others. John, Carol and the CTF family have an excellent track record of discipling their people. If the only outcome of this movement of God was the softening of my image of God, I could have remained rebellious, unaccountable, and not in charge of my own responses. I could have gone on behaving the way I had always behaved. Thankfully there were thousands of people across the world who had an encounter with The Father's Blessing and were deeply changed to be sons and daughters.

The Nicene Creed is the only creed accepted by all mainline Christian churches throughout the world. This creed mentions both a catholic and an apostolic church. The fact that the Church is apostolic is broadly accepted, but what does apostolic mean? For me, the word *apostolic* means a few different things, but primarily it means the church is based on a spirit of sonship. Signs and wonders are not the main point; they are an overflow of the spirit of sonship. We are the Church of Jesus Christ, a Son who was given to us. The Holy Spirit who birthed the church at Pentecost and who dwells within every believer is the Spirit of adoption, through whom we as sons can cry out, "Abba, Father." He is the same Spirit that gives witness to us that we are children of God. We are born again by the Spirit, this Holy Spirit of adoption, and I wonder how much of our Christian lives are spent at war with our identities as sons and daughters of God. A true apostolic church is not determined by what we do or what we call our leaders; it is determined by who we are and how we show up in our lives. The apostolic is a mindset focused on sonship. The government of heaven that Jesus created on earth is the five-fold ministry of apostles, prophets, pastors, teachers, and evangelists. The men and women who function in these roles must show up in their role as sons and daughters, not as Lords and Masters. Leaders in church are instructed to not lord it over people as often happens in the systems of this world.

The Prodigal Son

And He said, "A man had two sons. The younger of them said to his father, 'Father, give me the share of the estate that falls to me.' So he divided his wealth between them. And not many days later, the younger son gathered everything together and went on a journey into a distant country, and there he squandered his estate with loose living. Now when he had spent everything, a severe famine occurred in that country, and he began to be impoverished. So he went and hired himself out to one of the citizens of that country, and he sent him into his fields to feed swine. And he would have gladly filled his stomach with the pods that the swine were eating, and no one was giving anything to him. But when he came to his senses, he said, 'How many of my father's hired men have more than enough bread, but I am dying here with hunger! I will get up and go to my father, and will say to him, "Father, I have sinned against Heaven, and in your sight; I am no longer worthy to be called your son; make me as one of your hired men."' So he got up and came to his father. But while he was still a long way off, his father saw him and felt compassion for him, and ran and embraced him and kissed him. And the son said to him, 'Father, I have sinned against Heaven and in your sight; I am no longer worthy to be called your son.' But the father said to his slaves, 'Quickly bring out the best robe and put it on him, and put a ring on his hand and sandals on his feet; and bring the fattened calf, kill it, and let us eat and celebrate; for this son of mine was dead and has come to life again; he was lost and has been found.' And they began to celebrate.

"Now his older son was in the field, and when he came and approached the house, he heard music and dancing. And he summoned one of the servants and began inquiring what these things could be. And he said to him, 'Your brother has come, and your father has killed the fattened calf because he has received him back safe and sound.' But he became angry and was not willing to go in; and his father came out and began pleading with him. But he answered and said to his father, 'Look! For so many years I have been serving you and I have never neglected a command of yours; and yet you have never given me a young goat, so that I might celebrate with my friends; but when this son of yours came, who has de-

voured your wealth with prostitutes, you killed the fattened calf for him.' And he said to him, 'Son, you have always been with me, and all that is mine is yours. But we had to celebrate and rejoice, for this brother of yours was dead and has begun to live, and was lost and has been found'" (Luke 15:11–32).

There are five manifestations of sons in this passage. The first is that the father considered both his sons as sons. It didn't matter how they behaved or related to him, they were still his sons. Asking a spiritual father if he considers you a son is not the question you should ask. What someone else sees as your identity does not mean that is how you are behaving. You only get to be in charge of how you are responding as a son or daughter. It is quite likely that the disconnect you may feel, which is the likely motivation behind asking a question like this, will be found in your own heart and not the opinion of your spiritual father or mother.

The second is a son who has a spirit of entitlement. He comes to his father and says, "Give me what is mine to do with as I please." There is such danger in this heart posture growing in the grace and charismatic community right now. Princes and princesses are not taught entitlement; they are taught that as nobles they have certain responsibilities to steward well what has been given to them and to be thankful. Entitlement is selfish and will make us poor. We do not demand from God what He has provided for us. We do not sulk or pout because His time frame is different from ours. Sonship is not about getting to do what you want when you want to do it.

The third son to manifest is the son who is a servant in his heart. This is the person who expects to get what he worked for. Despite the father's wealth being divided between both his sons, this type of son never feels it was enough. It says, "I have done all you asked, worked diligently, and never neglected a command of yours, and you have never done a thing for me the way you are for this loser brother of mine." This elder brother is all too common in churches throughout the USA. Expectations of promotion because we have been doing something for years and then getting upset when someone who has never served the way we have is placed as an elder or leader really tests the elder brother in us all. If the blessings we have been praying for are given to the church down the street and it has a bunch of bitter and angry people that speak badly against me, then any trace of the elder brother in me will be provoked to the surface.

Next comes the son who will show up in his life as a hired hand, the one who is resigned to just being a servant in his father's house. Resigned to the fact that they will never amount to anything more, these sons settle in their hearts that they will do what is necessary, work for their wage, and nothing more. They have no big dreams, maybe just a flicker of hope that they will have some dignity restored by their hard work and gifting. The church has manifested this spirit and called it service. I do not want a spirit of service in the church I steward; I want a spirit of sonship. Service says, "I showed up, did what was asked, and I am done. You're welcome." The spirit of sonship asks, "What's next?" because sons and daughters know everything they work for will one day be passed onto them through the inheritance from their father and mother. A hired hand will never receive an inheritance. It is a poison in the church. Neither the hired hand nor the elder brother ever understands or receives the heart of their father. They want a list to check off and prove to some wounded self-esteem that they did what was required, that therefore nothing in their life, their ministry, or their relationship with their father could be their fault. Hired hands have zero expectation of favor and are looking for ways to be offended.

"This resurrection life you received from God is not a timid, grave-tending life. It's adventurously expectant, greeting God with a childlike 'What's next, Papa?' God's Spirit touches our spirits and confirms who we really are. We know who He is, and we know who we are: Father and children. And we know we are going to get what's coming to us — an unbelievable inheritance!" (Romans 8:15–16 The Message).

Then there is the son who understands sonship. The son who has a ring placed on his finger and sandals on his feet. If the cry of the older brother is "This isn't fair," the cry of the son is "I love my father and I am so thankful for everything." The son is connected to the heart of his father. He is not seeking what he can gain from his father but pursuing his father's heart. He understands that he will work from a place of favor and not for a place of favor. He works from a relationship and not for one. A son is responsible for his heart and for how it is connected to the heart of his father.

The striking difference between the heart of a son and the heart of an elder brother is that a son submits. *Submit* is probably the most hated word in the dictionary. The devil has sold us a bill of goods when it comes to submission. Husbands have bullied their wives, telling them it's the will of God that they submit. Church leaders have manipulated their congregations by telling them to submit. The definition of submission has come to mean that I am less than you—but that doesn't make sense. Jesus is not, was not, and never will be less than the Father, yet time and again He says He submits. The

Father gave us His Son, and the Son submitted. Jesus only did what He saw the Father doing, He could do nothing in Himself, He asked if there was any way other than crucifixion, and He submitted to His Father's will. Submission is not about being less than, it is simply a posture of being truly humble and laying down our lives for another.

None of us would have a relationship with Jesus if it were not for submission. Jesus submitted to being born and to dying, and when He reached out to us, we submitted ourselves to Him. Just because the Discipleship Movement got so much of this wrong (in my opinion that was because it emphasized the shepherd and not the sheep, the fathers and the not sons) does not mean it was all wrong. Submission is not about telling people who to marry and whose lawn to mow. Those are scary things. But it is vitally important to submit because Jesus submitted. When we are afraid that the person at the pulpit is teaching submission because he or she wants to have a mindless drone doing his or her will, our fear does not nullify truth. What if the authority Jesus gives is given to the measure you live in submission? The centurion understood authority and recognized it in Jesus. I often call older men "Sir." I get asked all the time if I was in the military. People under authority, those used to living in submission to authority, recognize others who do the same. And every soldier knows that when you are in submission to authority you get to use that authority. Who you submit to determines the authority you will flow in.

Sinn Fein is the political party of the Irish Republican Army in both North and South Ireland. *Sinn fein* is Gaelic for "ourselves alone." There is such a spirit of *sinn fein* throughout the church that we somehow think the highest form of discipleship is to do life on our own and submit to no one. "No one will take away my independence" and "No one will tell me what to do" are hallmark beliefs of the entitled, orphans, elder brothers, and hired hands. There has never been a time when God has not used the voice of a man or woman to speak to the earth. There has always been a prophetic spokesperson of God on earth. Our problem is that many of us want to be that voice. We want to be God's voice on earth and are not prepared to submit to the voice of another. We want to be a father or mother, but we just don't like being sons or daughters. This is a manifestation of the orphan spirit, as seen in the son who felt entitled, the son who was an elder brother, and the son who settled for being a hired hand. This orphan spirit also manifests in comments like "If you give me a good father, I will be a good son."

I am about to get into trouble with all the spiritual orphans out there who move from one church to another, listen to their favorite speaker from a church thousands of miles away, and wish they could have a church like that in their town—the orphans who don't get their way in their churches and see nothing but faults, or magnify and uncover the faults of their leaders and go off to start their own ministries in the hope that they will find happiness in being "ourselves alone." They may relate to other orphans desperate to find legitimacy, but all the time they are running from hearing the truth I am about to share. It is the heart of the son and not the heart of the father that brings breakthrough and favor. It's not the quality of fathering that matters; it is the quality of sonship. You are not in control of your spiritual fathers and mothers. You are only in control of you, which means you can decide to eat the fruit from a forbidden tree if you believe the lies of the enemy.

It is always easier to "submit" to a leader who doesn't know you and who lives hundreds of miles away than it is to submit to your own pastor. I remember a conversation I had with Bethel Church's Senior Associate Kris Vallotton—my only conversation with him in fact—and he said this: "People think we honor Bill [Johnson] because he is a great leader. The truth is Bill is a great leader because we honor him." Bill is a father to thousands across the world because he has people in his life who have decided they will be a son or daughter to him, they have submitted to him, and they serve him.

When I allow my heart posture to be reliant on the behavior of another person, I have let someone control me. To be clear, if someone scares you, you shouldn't be their son or daughter—but you should submit to someone who scares you a little. It should be a good scary. You will be corrected, and we often find correction scary, but it is the mark in Scripture of whether you are legitimate or illegitimate. You will be asked to do things you feel you are not qualified for, and that is good scary!

Sonship brings freedom. Jesus was the most free person on the planet, and yet we have this notion that submission brings bondage. Jesus came as a son, He ministered as a son, He died as a son, and He was resurrected as a son. His disciples followed Him by becoming sons. Being a son for all of them meant this: I will lay down my agenda and my life for the sake of yours. In becoming last, they became first; in becoming the least, they became the greatest. Many of us are content to lead small ministries having some impact, but if we understood and practiced submission, we would be leading nations.

I have had dozens of conversations with people who tell me God is their father and they need no other expression of that here on earth. That sounds so biblically honorable, but it's sheer nonsense. As I mentioned earlier, God has always used people to communicate His heart on earth, and we get to choose to submit to that or not. If that isn't good enough, then how did Jesus behave on earth? He behaved on earth in the same way

He did in heaven: He submitted. It is in the Bible if you don't believe me.

Visit to Jerusalem

Now His parents went to Jerusalem every year at the Feast of the Passover. And when He became twelve, they went up there according to the custom of the Feast; and as they were returning, after spending the full number of days, the boy Jesus stayed behind in Jerusalem. But His parents were unaware of it, but supposed Him to be in the caravan, and went a day's journey; and they began looking for Him among their relatives and acquaintances. When they did not find Him, they returned to Jerusalem looking for Him. Then, after three days they found Him in the temple, sitting in the midst of the teachers, both listening to them and asking them questions. And all who heard Him were amazed at His understanding and His answers. When they saw Him, they were astonished; and His mother said to Him, "Son, why have You treated us this way? Behold, Your father and I have been anxiously looking for You." And He said to them, "Why is it that you were looking for Me? Did you not know that I had to be in My Father's house?" But they did not understand the statement that He had made to them. And He went down with them and came to Nazareth, and He continued in subjection to them; and His mother treasured all these things in her heart. And Jesus kept increasing in wisdom and stature, and in favor with God and men" (Luke 2:41–52).

Did you get that last piece? Jesus "continued in subjection to them." That word "subjection" is the Greek word *hypotassō* and means to submit to and to place oneself under the authority of. Here was King Jesus, doing what was in His heart to do—a mission given from the Father, learning and enlightening His people about the deep truths of heaven. If that were most of us, we would see Mary and Joseph as agents of the devil sent to delay and thwart God's will in our lives. We would see them as people who would stop the great mission we have been called to, but Jesus submitted to them. Mary knew what was happening and treasured this moment in her heart. Jesus, God's Son who did not consider the equity He had with God something to be utilized, the One in whom the fullness of the Godhead bodily dwelt, said yes to His earthly mother and father. And remember Joseph was only His father because Jesus decided that is who Joseph would be to Him, and in this passage Joseph is actually called Jesus' father. Jesus had a completely justifiable reason to not call Joseph His father, but He did and submitted to Joseph.

What we say manifests in our vertical relationship with heaven should manifest in our horizontal relationships on earth. If we say we are sons and daughters of our Father in heaven, it should be recognizable by those near us because it will manifest as us being son and daughters on earth. Jesus needed to grow in wisdom, stature, and grace (favor) with God and men, and He did it by manifesting His sonship horizontally. Do you want more favor on your life? Do you want men to say you are fit for your purpose (stature)? Then grow in your horizontal sonship. Learn to submit.

Jack Frost said it well:

"Have you wondered why you have not seen more lasting fruit in your life? Do you wonder why you don't have more influence in your workplace? Do you wonder why you haven't come into the place that God has called you to in your local church and that you know He wants you to move into? Are you sowing into your inheritance? Or do you cop an

attitude when it's time to take up an offering or to bless your pastor or boss at Christmastime? He who is faithful in a very little thing is faithful also in much; and he who is unrighteous in a very little thing is unrighteous also in much... And if you have not been faithful in the use of that which is another's, who will give you that which is your own? (Luke 16:10,12 NAS). Your inheritance, the word God has given you, is delayed until you learn obedience from the things that you suffer by becoming a son or a daughter. Then you begin to become a representative of God's transforming love to your family and others. It is all wrapped up in the principles of honor and submission, of humbling yourself to become faithful with that which is another's, of getting underneath and pushing up, of serving unselfishly and wholeheartedly to build up another with no personal agenda or ulterior motives."

Frost, Jack (2006-11-28). Spiritual Slavery to Spiritual Sonship (pages 203–204). Destiny Image.

What you do with that which belongs to another is the guiding principle of Kingdom increase. We are content to be baptized with the sufferings of Jesus as long as there are people rejecting us because of our weird behavior or our conservative beliefs, but we balk at being baptized by His true suffering—learning to submit. It is a daily cross, a daily suffering. Jesus only suffered at the hands of Pilate for a day or two. This kind of suffering and laying down our lives for the sake of another is required each and every day, but it comes with the promise of abundance and increase. I get to decide how much blessing I want in my life by having the posture of a heart that submits.

Orphan Thinking

As I previously mentioned, my dad died when I

was 11 years old, just four weeks shy of my 12th birthday. I can remember being angry at him for not waiting around until my birthday. After all, he had just celebrated my brother's birthday. Why couldn't he have waited for mine? We were pretty poor, so five months later at the ripe age of 12, I got a job. I worked between 12 and 40 hours a week to support myself and help out at home. Many of my mom's friends would tell me what a great kid I was, working to help out. I worked every school break and have never had a summer off since 1976. I just worked. I was able to buy my own clothes, I didn't need pocket money like my older brother, and I was also able to buy my mom things. What a hero!

Except none of that was motivated by a healthy identity. In my heart, I knew no one would rescue me, no one would help me, and if something had to be done, I would need to do it myself. Life was hard, unjust, and unfair, and I needed to "cowboy up" and take some responsibility. I call that developing an orphan heart.

I think we all have orphan hearts and most of us can accurately diagnose it in others, believing we have dealt with our own. The problem with this is that in Scripture, when we see a speck in someone's eye it usually means there is a bigger manifestation of the exact same thing in our own. The greater fault is mine, not what I see in you. Most of us have not really dealt with orphan thinking; we have learned how to manage it. In my life, this has been a process. In 1994 I was radically impacted by the message of the Father's love. In 2003 Jack Frost prayed for me in Toronto. In 2007 I had my experience at Bethel and bought Jack's book. I read it and thought it would be great for many people I knew: it could really help them. Then in 2008, after sitting at the table where my leaders affirmed me as their father, I read the book again and started to really get it. And when it got a hold of me, it deeply got a hold of me.

I believe every problem on earth can be attributed to the absence of sonship and the manifestation of an orphan heart. It's the same heart present in the elder brother, the hired hand, and the entitled heir. Jack Frost describes the process of becoming an orphan or developing an orphan heart. I have come to prefer the term orphan heart because when people talk about an orphan spirit it can give the false impression that it can be cast out. Unfortunately, it can't be cast out—but it can be untrained and dealt with, which is often a process of unlearning and learning.

In his book *Spiritual Slavery to Spiritual Sonship*, Jack Frost outlines 12 steps to the path of an orphan heart. It's a fantastic read and very insightful. I think all 12 steps boil down to one simple thing: being offended. Then we dig into our offense and cultivate it. We are even taught in some circles that we should be offended—offended at sin, political decisions, and people who believe things we don't or emphasize things we don't. It even goes into racism; we put up signs to stop mostly young black men from sagging! Offense is often seen as a mark of deep spiritual maturity, but I want to say it is a sign you don't know God very well and it's an indicator of immaturity. Most of us come in pretty broken, and when we find a church, we have a tendency to place the pastor, leader, or at least someone who befriended us on a pedestal. The elation of finding a place to call home, to find family in a local church, is one of those moments in life that is sweetly divine. After a while though, someone will get noticed more than me or the leader will walk past me and not even smile.

I once wore a replica of a CCCP T-shirt from the time period when the USSR was opening up to bands in the 80s and someone got offended and left the church. They didn't even let me know until a couple of years later. They did let others know though, probably so they would pray for my soul. The thing about being offended is that it is usually completely justified. I don't know if you know this, but the church is led by imperfect people. I have given people plenty of opportunity to be offended and many have taken that opportunity and bolted, all for good reasons. It just isn't the way of the Kingdom. The way of the Kingdom is to consider others more important than ourselves. It is this attitude that drives the son or daughter. There is a peculiar story in John 2.

On the third day there was a wedding in Cana of Galilee, and the mother of Jesus was there; and both Jesus and His disciples were invited to the wedding. When the wine ran out, the mother of Jesus said to Him, "They have no wine." And Jesus said to her, "Woman, what does that have to do with us? My hour has not yet come." His mother said to the servants, "Whatever He says to you, do it." Now there were six stone waterpots set there for the Jewish custom of purification, containing twenty or thirty gallons each. Jesus said to them, "Fill the waterpots with water." So they filled them up to the brim. And He said to them, "Draw some out now and take it to the headwaiter." So they took it to him. When the headwaiter tasted the water which had become wine, and did not know where it came from (but the servants who had drawn the water knew), the headwaiter called the bridegroom, and said to him, "Every man serves the good wine first, and when the people have drunk freely, then he serves the poorer wine; but you have kept the good wine until now." This beginning of His signs Jesus did in Cana of Galilee, and manifested His glory, and His disciples believed in Him (John 2:1–11).

Here is a story of people at a wedding, drinking so much wine that they run out, and Jesus makes them more wine—the kind that is good enough to astound the waiter. The word translated here as "the people have drunk freely" actually means "to be drunk" and was used as a metaphor for murder. These people were killing the wine! But that should not be the most puzzling part of this miracle. Jesus clearly told his mother, Mary, that the time for His ministry to go public was not now. Jesus Himself told the disciples in John 5:19 that He could do nothing in Himself; He could only do what He saw the Father doing. The Father obviously wasn't changing water into wine, and there is no trace of Jesus even doubting this. Yet He did it. He did what His mother asked Him to do.

By Jesus being a son on earth, He shifted heaven and brought His time forward. When we submit; when we lay our bags at someone's feet, when we lay our lives, callings, and dreams down for the sake of making another greater, we will be released sooner than we anticipate and we will move in our Kingdom anointing. Jesus learned this as a 12-year-old and had no trouble manifesting it as a 30-year-old. Jesus showing up as a son to Mary on earth is what moved the Father in heaven to propel Jesus into His public ministry in Cana, where Jesus did many signs and won the hearts of His disciples. This was all because He did not get offended by the presumption of His mother. He didn't respond with some version of "You don't control me, Mother!" And He didn't use revelation or some great big spiritual reason as an excuse. It is the heart of the son or daughter that brings breakthrough and favor; it isn't the heart of the father or mother.

Offense is in the heart of every orphan out there. Some spend their lives looking to be offended, waiting for the opportunity to blame, complain, and justify why their lives are stuck and it isn't their fault. Others have such thin skins that the moment anyone mentions something around their weak spots, they retreat into hurt and offense, blaming anyone: "No one understands me. No one has the kids I have, the parents I had, the stuff going on in my life." The cry of the orphan heart looks for ways not to take responsibility. Somehow it is easier to be stuck than to get unstuck.

Becoming a son or daughter is an exercise in throwing off the shackles of victimhood, taking responsibility for your life and needs, and walking in favor. I don't believe it's the Jezebel spirit, the Leviathan spirit, the Python spirit or any of these "spirits" that oppose the church as much as the orphan spirit. This spirit is the root of all division, dissension, and ultimately divorce that happens among churches and relationships. The rejection of leadership under the smoke screens of control, manipulation, and failure all put the blame on the other and give the "victim" an excuse to walk away, be disconnected, and never trust again. God gave us a Son. A Son was born to us. A Son died on the cross for the sake of His Father's wishes.

The moments of my greatest failings, those times when I have been so bitter, angry, resentful, and have walked away from relationships, have been those moments when my little orphan has led the way in my life. It has always delayed my destiny. Some seem very keen to embrace a life of suffering, believing it is good and that because Jesus suffered we should also. After all, we are told in Philippians that we will suffer and Paul prayed that we would be baptized with Jesus' sufferings. What I find weird is that we are willing to suffer in ways Jesus never suffered, and we resist the suffering Jesus actually endured. We embrace sickness as God's hand to teach us things. If sickness is from God and is the key to supernatural breakthrough, then Jesus should have been the sickest person on earth. We embrace the suffering of isolation and going it alone, when Jesus had close friends and family with Him to the sweet glorious end.

Every leader in your life, every representation of authority, will let you down. They will be imperfect and they will hurt you. It will most likely not be intentional on their part, but sometimes when you make a decision, you know it will hurt someone—and yet you still have to make the decision. The key is not to become offended when someone does hurt you or lets you down.

Submit and Obey

Obey your leaders and submit to them, for they keep watch over your souls as those who will give an account. Let them do this with joy and not with grief, for this would be unprofitable for you (Hebrews 13:17).

Submission and obedience to leaders are good for you. Of course they are good for your leaders as they get to experience joy and don't need to sigh and groan, but submission and obedience are primarily for the benefit of those who submit. Submission is a matter of the heart, and obedience is a matter of behavior. Both are required. Instances abound throughout Scripture of men and women of God submitting to and being obedient to ungodly masters. I would argue that submission is always required, but obedience is not required when to do so would mean being disobedient to God. Shadrack, Meshack, and Abednego all maintained a posture of submission to an evil king but refused to be obedient when it violated the rule of God. Their conduct in the third chapter of Daniel tells us they remained submissive to Nebuchadnezzar, calling him "O king" on more than one occasion, but they remained unwilling to obey when it violated their worship of the One true King.

If a leader requires me to wear a suit, I should have

a good attitude about it and be obedient. If a leader requires me to fall down and worship him or her, I should still have a good attitude to them, but refuse on the grounds that it violates my higher obedience. At no time am I permitted to call leaders idiots, malign their character, or make things up about their intentions and motives.

In the church we are often so afraid of partnering darkness with light that we jump straight to coming out from among them as instructed in 2 Corinthians 6. But I want to suggest that we jump too early and in the wrong direction. If someone asks me to violate God's Word, I should respectfully, honorably decline because disrespect and dishonor are darkness and do not exist in heaven. Sure, the systems of this world are filled with disrespect and dishonor, yet we are told to honor the king. We are told to do this by Peter, the man who saw James beheaded by the king and who was personally imprisoned by the same king, presumably to be beheaded also. Coming out from among them is about not behaving with the best darkness the world offers and calling it godly. It is not operating from a political or religious spirit, but operating from a posture of true humility and honoring the God-given government and rule. It is not compromising on the standards of love, faithfulness, and honor. I would argue that instead of not being like those unaffected by the culture of heaven, we mostly tend to behave and react in exactly the same way.

Sonship is *the* secret sauce of Greater Chicago Church. You cannot have a Spirit of adoption without sonship. Sonship is the primary heart posture that shapes our character and transforms us into His image. It's no wonder it has been so attacked by our enemy.

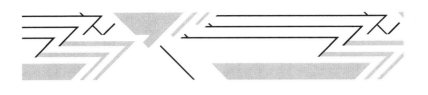

3

Angels

I always tell people that I never travel alone. I am keenly aware of my angelic companions. The title for this section could be something along the lines of "Things I believe will get me locked up, medicated, or have the heretic hunters hunt me down with pitchforks and burning lanterns." I believe in angels and I believe in our interaction with them. I can also see them.

The word "angel" appears 187 times in the New Testament. A simple reading of the Gospels will show you how angels work. They appear, stir waters for healing, prophesy over people, speak and converse with people, minister and strengthen people, release people from prison, and prepare people for their destinies.

When I was a child, I grew up in a very superstitious home. God didn't exist for us. Even though we were forced to go to a Church of Ireland Sunday School for a while, I honestly knew nothing about God. I thought it was normal to have Jesus and Santa Claus mixed up, as long as you knew Santa was more important because he brought you stuff. My paternal grandmother talked to leprechauns, believed her dead husband appeared to her all the time in the form of a blackbird, and could foretell people's deaths by listening to her family banshee. Some children placed their teeth under their pillows for the tooth fairy, but we hung ours on a fairy tree at the bottom of her garden. (Leprechauns and banshees are Irish fairies—but much more mean than the Tinkerbell type!)

My maternal grandmother was blind and a fanatical knitter. She knitted all our sweaters in patterns that she would follow by touch. She even at times included different colors of wool to form lines and patterns in the sweater. Let me be clear: she was completely physically blind, unable to distinguish between light and dark. She wouldn't know if the lights were on or off. But she did know who walked in the room before they made a sound, and I even remember her telling me that something was wrong with my clothing. Her ability to "see" was off the charts. When I moved to the USA, my mom would call me from 4,000 miles away when she knew something was wrong. She was correct 99% of the time. During some of the darkest times here, she would call because she sensed things were off somehow. There was a lot of spiritual activity in my childhood home, and my mom and grandmother seemed comfortable with it.

For years as a child, I had a figure that stood in my bedroom almost every night. It was about three feet tall, wore a dark hat and a dark cloak, and had piercing orange eyes that (thankfully!) it kept closed most of the time. I was not afraid of it but remember being slightly unnerved and I was really thankful on the rare nights it wasn't there. I remember my grandmother telling me that we didn't know if it was good or bad so let it be—don't disturb it. We were always encouraged to welcome ghosts or spirits into the room when a breeze blew through the room or a door opened by itself.

What does all this have to do with angels? Stated very simply, I see the seer gift as an extension of discernment. The seer knows what is going on in the spiritual realm and the ability to see is often passed on from generation to generation. There are people groups all over the word that have moved for generations in revelatory gifts. The Irish are, in my opinion, some of the most discerning people in the world and have a rich tradition both inside and outside of the Kingdom of knowing what is happening in the spiritual realm. This has been the source of much conflict simply because we all think we "know" what is really going on. Of course this gift of "knowing" has been misapplied and misappropriated for a different kingdom. Spirits, ghosts, and apparitions are all too common a way of life for a lot of Irish people. I suspect it is true for other Celts and other people groups as well.

The good thing is many of us have been raised in an environment where we accept the mysterious nature of the spirit realm and how it interacts with us on a daily basis. The bad thing is that the spirit realm is often confined to dark places, dark beliefs, and devilish systems. The human system tends to see the realm of the spiritual as a mental illness, mere hallucinations that children will hopefully grow out of. Scripture seems to see it as perfectly normal. The church has long been suspicious of the spiritual realm: it has either seen it as being completely from the devil or it has been so marginalized that it's only the "weirdo" who has encounters with the visible, manifest spirit realm. Don't get me wrong. The mentally ill do exist and the spirit realm often manipulates them. Some people just make things up, while others have experiences that are unhelpful at best or demonic at worst.

When I mention that I see in the spirit realm, people respond in one of a few ways. They often ask me if I can see their angel. Ninety-nine percent of the time I tell them it doesn't work like that. Or they get freaked out and compartmentalize this part of me because their experience of this realm has been learned through movies, books, and rumors.

Let me explain how it works for me. Most of the time, I live in a normal five-senses realm. Occasionally I get what I call "interrupted" by the spirit realm. For example, for a number of months I saw chariots race down streets and highways. These were the stereotypical Roman chariots as seen in the movie *Ben Hur*. They were driven by angels and pulled by what looked like horses. On more than one occasion I have hit the brakes in my vehicle to avoid them because they were so real. On other occasions, I have been completely distracted by the movement of angels in a specific location. This happens frequently at dawn or dusk, times when the changing light requires us to focus a little differently and it can be easier to "see." Driving to Bethel Church in Redding has always been very distracting for me simply because the angelic activity is astoundingly active, especially when leaders are gathering.

If I want to "tap into" the seer realm, I need to activate it. In my experience, examining myself, my motives, and my heart helps activate the gift, and I can switch it on. The heart piece has been especially crucial. Years ago I would activate it from a place of impurity, often the desire to judge something or someone. I believe that judgment is the enemy and blockage to seeing in the spirit. I often do not have permission to see things and I always ask the Father if it is okay for me to interact with the spirit realm. If I were to force the issue, much like Saul forcing the issue to summon Samuel from the dead, it would be a violation of the gift.

I cannot stress this part enough. Judgment is the enemy of operating in the revelatory gifts. In my experience and reading of Scripture, the reason to see is so we can understand what heaven is doing, not what the enemy is doing. This allows us to partner with God's plans and purposes. Too often we have either seen or encouraged people to see what the enemy is doing so we can react. At my core, I believe that we are not called to react to the enemy but to partner with heaven. Jesus said He would build His church and the gates of hell would not prevail. I don't want to see what the gates of hell are doing; I want to see what God is doing. If we surrender judgment and if we focus on understanding what God is doing, we can see, feel, and discern what the angels are about.

I have known my personal angel since 2008. I first met him (and he is sitting beside me as I type this right now) at our church during a 24-hour prayer meeting. My wife Rachel and I had brought our three kids to the prayer meeting, and they were reluctant to say the least. I suspect all parents have endured times when our kids do not want to do something, we make them do it and we endure the moaning, complaining, and ensuing resistance that follows. I was distracted and not engaged with what was happening at the meeting. I decided to focus my heart on heaven and God—and in a moment, I saw two angels at the front of the church. I had never done this before but I asked the Father if I could talk with them, and He said yes. I went to the first one and asked him his name. He told me he was called "Righteous." I asked him what he was there for. He stood by the north wall of our church building and told me he was there to make sure none of the accusations from inside or outside the church would stick to us. As he spoke, he touched the wall and it looked like a Teflon-like substance was left behind.

I then moved to the next angel and asked him his name. At first he was silent. I asked him his name again, and he told me he was called "Valor." I asked him what that meant. He said, "Courage gets you to a fight, but valor is what makes your hand freeze to the sword." It was a reference to the scripture of David's mighty men who fought so hard their hands froze to their swords. Valor has been with me ever since. Righteous moved on. I think he was with us in the early days of our transition because he needed to establish something, but Valor is still with me. He talks with me, is with me when I play golf or go hiking, and the thought of him leaving or being reassigned makes me sad to the point of tears. He is that real.

In 2014, my wife and I went to Dubai enroute to the vacation of lifetime in the Maldives. As I walked through the airport, Valor appeared on my right and he was absolutely hyper. He had not been in Dubai before and was loving the mixture of cultures. Later on this same vacation, as I sat on the porch overlooking the Indian Ocean, he came and brought some friends with him. We had a party, and I thought they were being so loud they would wake everyone up, including my sleeping wife. I was overcome by the Spirit and the presence of God the whole evening and spent the night on the hammock praising and glorifying Jesus. I asked Valor if he would be okay with me interviewing him for this book, and he has agreed, but first let me tell you some more stories.

Our church in Oak Park is the only building we own at the moment, and it has two *huge* seraphim. I see them as being red, but others do not. It is important to know that seers often do not align with details but do align with major themes. We have had lots of people see these two angels, unprompted. They arrived on Pentecost 2010.

At the Pastors and Leaders Conference at Catch The Fire in Toronto, I had seen an enormous shimmering angel at the front of the church sanctuary. I asked the Father if I could talk with the angel, and the Father seemed to indicate that I could try. I approached the angel and asked him his name. He ignored me. I asked the Father again and was told to go ahead. This time the angel told me his name and it was something indecipherable. He did not look at me. I asked him what he was there for and he told me *they* were the "Guardians of the Presence." At that, I looked where he was looking across the auditorium, and I could see a very similar angel. They locked eyes with each other and he said they were present in CTF Toronto to guard the presence of God that was so highly valued by John and Carol Arnott. I asked if our church had similar angels and he said, "Not yet, but they will arrive" and gave me the date. Sure enough, on that date, two seraphim arrived at Greater Chicago Church. There was no earthquake, no shattering of windows, and no sound of trumpets, but they arrived and have remained with us since.

It is so important to note that angels are all around us, though we often do not notice when they are around, at least not immediately. We do sometimes notice when their assignment increases. Often with this, our awareness of their presence becomes greater and our engagement with the given assignment increases. Angels are on assignment. If the minister or church does not engage with that assignment, they become unemployed and often can be assigned elsewhere. (That is not the case for those with territorial assignment.) I frequently see angels sitting on church buildings, doing nothing. I have asked what this is about, and I have been told that often there is an assignment or a mantle that is given to a church and it is refused, ignored, or the people quit because it is too difficult. The angels posted on such assignments are left hanging until someone with the authority to do it steps up and takes ownership of it.

We have an angel at our house. He is about 5'8" tall, wears normal clothes, and is almost always reading. He doesn't like to be in the same room as we are in and will often leave a room when anyone walks in. He will stand on the stairs and wait for us to go to bed or go to the basement. If he is in the basement when we go there to watch TV, he will leave. He doesn't speak to anyone, but his assignment is protection and peace. Angels always have an assignment. Sometimes they are new to their assignment and will have to learn and grow just as we do. As they get more established in doing what they are called to do, they get confident and bigger. Sometimes their assignments change. For example, if an angel has an assignment of healing, they may be reassigned to a person or place that needs help with miracles. Angels will be able to apply what they know in a new place and grow in a new assignment. They normally grow with the person they are assigned to, day by day, battle by battle. It is important to note that angels do not make things easy, they just make things possible.

Frequently as I preach, an angel joins me. He normally stands on my left and ministers to the congregation with whatever I am preaching about. He isn't there all the time but shows up when something is about to shift. At one recent meeting while I was preaching, I sensed God wanted to break off some depression and bondage from the congregation. At that, I was joined by dozens of angels who all drew weapons. As people stood for ministry, I released the angels and they began striking spirits of depression and bondage off people. It was a very powerful time of ministry.

One time I took our youth group on our annual trip to a huge youth conference at Toronto Airport Christian Fellowship (now Catch The Fire). The Christian band

Delirious was playing and we were right up front, worshiping with abandon. At one point, the atmosphere became very tender and many—including me—were on our knees worshiping. I then heard a noise like a soccer chant. "Ole, ole, ole. Ole. Ole." I thought a youth group had gotten out of hand and was interrupting the deep worship happening, but people were worshiping even more, and greater levels of intimacy seemed to be happening all around. I looked up and saw a band of angels "hanging off" the balcony, jubilantly chanting for a winning team.

Jesus Culture, a ministry started at Bethel Church, Redding, came to Chicago in August 2011. On the last night of the event something amazing happened. Banning Liebscher went on stage to close worship and transition into ministry. At least he tried to. As he began to speak, there was a massive influx of angels. Some people near me felt something brushing against them. I had never seen anything like it. The angels were manic—flying, looping the loop, swarming. Then the congregation continued in worship, spontaneous in what sounded like a Native American chant. People were on their feet giving glory to Jesus, and suddenly the angels gathered, created an open space in their midst, and fell into lines like an army. When they made space, in came the angel of Chicago. He was massive. The worship intensified even more and this angel, bigger than any I have ever seen, fell to his knees, a signal that every other angel followed. And in came Jesus. King Jesus in all His splendor entered the Allstate Arena and the place erupted with worship once more! I was undone.

Angels often respond to what they know is about to happen. They also direct things. One time I was at a Vineyard worship conference in Exeter, England with a Vineyard worship leader called Scott Underwood. Scott is an incredibly anointed worship leader from California and led a wonderful set of worship. We had been worshiping for "the usual" 40 minutes or so, and it became obvious that he was landing the worship plane. Near the ceiling of the room, I noticed two angels swirling in a circle (the way you would imagine sharks swirl around their intended prey). They looked at each other, smiled, nodded, and began speeding up, then began diving down and flying upwards. Well, the worship took off. People were weeping, dancing, and falling on their faces in the glory of the King. I spoke to Scott afterwards and he said he was coming to the close of worship, but he was aware that something shifted so he waited.

Angels are frequently engaged in spiritual warfare. I know people who have seen battles between angels and demons and they describe it as an almost medieval, Tolkienesque conflict—with swords, armor, etc. It is important for seers to know that what they see is a revelation requiring interpretation. The warfare angels engage in is primarily, but not exclusively, about truth and lies. Truth and lies are the foundation of the spirit world. We experience it as an "energy," an atmosphere created in the spirit realm that a lot of people are sensitive to. Most of us have walked in the halls of a hospital and "felt" despair, death, and sickness. An atmosphere has been created by what is believed and spoken or declared. Angels and demons battle over which atmosphere reigns in a place. I have seen angels with scars and dents on their armor. The swords they carry are representatives of the Word of God—the promises, hope, joy and redemption of God Himself. We can empower the angelic with our words and declarations, and we can empower the powers of darkness in the same way. This is why we can visit with someone and just feel icky. We don't rebuke the person; we submit to God, resist the atmosphere, and empower the truth.

Angels are not omnipresent. They don't go to the bathroom with you or hang out in your bedroom. They respect your privacy and engage with your assignment, not your intimacy.

Many of us expect angelic encounters to be ecstatic. We expect to shake, fall down, and remember these moments forever. That can certainly happen. Scripture is filled with such instances, but they are often seemingly normal moments. I am cautious when a seer has only ecstatic experiences with the angelic. It reminds me of when I first started to speak in tongues and thought it should be ecstatic all the time. Instead speaking in tongues is a decision I make to engage with God in a certain way. Like all gifts of the spirit, it is turned on by faith, not ecstasy.

Angels have personalities. I know this may be shocking. They are not robots, and they have a choice to follow God or not. That is why two thirds of them stayed with God while one third of them left with Satan. It seems even the good angels can get things wrong. We should never get our theology from an angel. Paul tells us in Galatians that even if an angel preaches a different gospel, we should curse it (Galatians 1:8).

I have asked the Father if it would be okay to interview Valor (my personal angel) for this book. I believe He said it was okay. Valor actually suggested it a few months ago and is very excited about it. He has a great sense of humor. I am a little nervous, not because of the interview, but because I have never wanted to be known as "the angel guy." People could either get weird or condemn me as being absurd or dangerous. I am also concerned about my reputation, as most people would be. I care about what those whom I respect and admire will think of me, and I won't pretend that I don't. However, I know part of the reason we are not seeing the Kingdom advance as we should is because we are not engaging with our angels. We tend to minimize the power of the spirit realm or hand it off to the evil one's disciples.

I am committed to calling the church into her fullness and activating her in partnering with the angelic. These are the ways of the angels: partnering with churches and leading in regions, breaking apostles out of prisons, warning of impending danger, bringing food and ministering to Jesus, reaping the harvest, coming with Jesus, causing the earth to quake and rolling away a stone, prophesying to us and coming with answers to our prayers, declaring the gospel of the Kingdom and the incarnation of Christ, strengthening Jesus in the garden, stirring up waters of healing, sitting where Jesus' body lay to announce the risen Lord, telling Phillip where to go to win the Ethiopian and thus a nation, telling a centurion to meet with Peter and thus being the catalyst for the gospel going to the Gentiles, and comforting Paul when he was shipwrecked.

We cannot ignore angels; nor are we to worship them. But we can talk with them. Mary did, Peter did, Zacharias did, Daniel did. The list goes on and on, and their conversations also are recorded. This interview is not infallible. Nothing I write is. This is my experience of talking to and interviewing my angel—a gift from God that has been so precious to me and that I am so grateful for.

Interview with an Angel

Ian: What is it like being an angel?

Valor: I know nothing else and would not want to know anything else except for one thing. You can know what it was like to have God send His Son, for God to become a child, live for you, die for you, and be resurrected for you. You can know what it is like for God to ascend and sit at the right hand of the Father for you, send His Spirit for you, and live inside of you. I will never know this. Sometimes it seems like most Christians don't know this! But we have gazed at His face for millennia. I bet you would like that. [He laughs.]

Ian: Yes I would—and I will! Do you experience God's love as we do?

Valor: God is love. He does not exist as another form and then decide to be loving. He is love. To be near Him is to know love—pure love. It is what causes me to shudder, to sing, to play, to dance. All I am is in response to knowing Him as love. His love is a fierce love, a love that causes life, causes galaxies, and causes beauty. It is a love that incites devotion.

Ian: Why are you given to us?

Valor: You know that one, Ian. We are sent on assignment. We have been given a mission that aligns with your mission. We are with you on co-mission. You like that, don't you? [laughter]. We are here to be on a mission or assignment with you, helping you do what you need heaven to do. We do not do what you can do; we only do what you need heaven's help to do.

Ian: Does everyone have an angel? And only one?

Valor: Yes and no. For those in the Kingdom, for those who have accepted the mission of the Kingdom, you have been given a job to do. It is based on the design God chose when He created you. If you accept the call, we are assigned. If that assignment changes, you can lose or increase your assigned angel or angels. Those who are not on a Kingdom assignment do not have an assigned angel, but sometimes the Father will send one of us to step in or help because it helps the Kingdom mission. Some have more than one angel, especially if they have multiple assignments or if they have a territorial mission. Sometimes the angel doesn't change but the minister does. For example, the angel of the USA has a fixed territorial assignment, at least until Texas secedes (Valor smiles), but he works with various people.

Ian: Do you take orders from men or just God?

Valor: We only take orders from God, but sometimes these orders come through people, often as God responds to prayer. I cannot tell you enough that we are here on assignment and will honor the assignment and respond to requests that further that assignment. We are activated through prophecy and declarations that are aligned with the will of the Father toward that assignment. We are made more powerful through these declarations when they have faith attached to them. You have seen the angel of Chicago. He lay dormant for years, around a hundred years or so, and was awakened in 2011 in response to the prayers of people about Chicago. He has been active, but people are largely misunderstanding what is happening.

Ian: What do you mean?

Valor: Christians get zealous when they sense something new is shifting. They think God is answering their prayers, which is part of it, but really He is answering the prayers of Jesus—the intercession of Jesus as He prays for the church. God is not making a place for individuals to be significant; He is making a place for the name of Jesus to be lifted high. The Name that's above all names. The Name that shouts from heaven a message of love, joy, and peace—not of striving, competition, and jealousy. Orphans in the church see these things as tolerable for the expansion of the Kingdom and their own promotion, but God will not move until the people He has chosen walk in the message He speaks. There is often a flurry of activity on the earth when an angel of this scale (like the angel of Chicago) is awakened. Some of it leads to confusion. The enemy also uses these times to increase his activity to divide, to discourage, and to destroy. The church in Chicago will increase in strength and authority as she begins to align with heaven through the message of Jesus and the government God has placed on earth.

Ian: Do you mean the five-fold?

Valor: That isn't heaven's term. We talk about God's government on earth, but it means the people God has assigned to bring heaven to earth legitimately.

Ian: Legitimately?

Valor: [Laughing] You know this, Ian.

Ian: I know. I am just asking for the record.

Valor: This is strange, but I will go over it. The anointing of priests used to be with oil. Since Jesus, it has been done by the laying on of hands. To lay hands on someone, you must carry the authority to do it. There has been a move to anoint by giving people a certificate, by giving them a degree, by attending a course, or by just calling yourself A, B, or C. These are all false. It's a false version of what you call five-fold. It is a false government built by people who think they are ministers of the gospel when they are really just good people doing good things that will not equip the saints to minister. It is like they are running in place, expending a lot of energy, and getting nowhere. They often get tired, worn out, and disappointed because they are independent from and often have rejected Jesus' gifts to the church.

Ian: Will that change, and if so, how?

Valor: It isn't important that it changes. What is important is that the real government of God for an assignment, a city, and a nation manifest and do what they are assigned to do. God will always bless His people, even those who are running in place, but it is of the utmost importance that the true government of heaven appears on earth.

Ian: How can we walk in more power from God?

Valor: Repent. [He laughs.] It is about changing your thinking and bringing alignment into your life from heaven to earth, in that order. Most of the stories about angels have no problem with seeing us as warriors—those who know authority and can move in authority. We take orders and give orders, just like the centurion you mentioned on Sunday. Yet you all seem to think or behave in a way that tells us you believe this is good for the angels, but a different set of rules apply to you. Heaven is a place of order, of rank or assignment. To grow in favor and influence, you must be aligned with your rank and your assignment, and that will mean you are under someone else's rank and assignment. When this alignment happens, the angels begin to vibrate. It is very empowering for us. Also, remember that you are blessed when you have a pure heart, and then you will see God. When you can align your heart around the values of heaven, you will see God. This is how you connect with the unseen as well—by turning your heart and will in alignment toward heaven.

Ian: What was it like when Satan fell?

Valor: It was the most stupid thing ever. There was instantly a different sound—a mixture of violence and seduction came from the Throne Room—and in a moment some had aligned with that sound and were cast out of heaven. As Jesus described, it was like a lightning bolt that expelled Satan and those who sang his melody of violence and seduction. They are the enemy and will be treated as the enemy. They chose and they chose wrong. On the day Jesus was crucified, they thought they had won, but we knew something else was going on. It wasn't a secret to any of us, but they were blinded by the violence and seduction and believed they had been victorious. But at the moment when Jesus cried, "It is done," all of heaven was filled with the power of God and the enemy was defeated. The battle wasn't even a close one. It wasn't the angels who were weeping in Revelation 5; it was John. He had to be told not to cry. We all knew it was Jesus who was about to show up. God always does what He says He will do. Always.

Ian: Is there anything that frustrates you?

Valor: A lot. [He laughs.]

Ian: Do you want to tell me more?

Valor: Not really. Frustration disappears when I see His face. When I hear the sound of Jesus, everything comes into order. Jesus is better than you could ever imagine. His voice calms storms and His laughter changes everything that hears it. Creation itself is restored by His laughter.

Ian: What would you like us to know?

Valor: We love beauty. We love creation. We love to play and have fun. We love to dance. In fact movement is one of the ways you can feel us and interpret what we are doing, especially during worship. Sometimes spontaneous dancers just mimic what we are doing without knowing it! Most of all, I wish you knew what He thinks of you. How He talks about you. How He loves you. You should hear how He brags about you, to us and all of heaven. I wish you knew how good He really is. He will gather all of heaven, all those who have gone to be with Him, all the saints who paid a price for the increase of His government, and He will point to you and go on and on about what a delight you are to Him. We never get tired of listening to a proud Father boasting about His children.

Ian: How do you cope with terrible injustice?

Valor: It is only unjust on earth. I have seen Him take the most terrible thing here on earth and turn it into the most beautiful thing in eternity. I would add to the previous question that I wish you knew this life is only a blade of grass, but there is a day that will come for every person who calls Jesus "Lord" when He will make it all not just as good as new, but way more wonderful than you could even imagine. There is a day when you will see His face and you will know He has not allowed you to lose a thing, but in fact you've gained more than you could ask or imagine. This life will pass and He will repay you. Every act of brutality and injustice will be compensated for in an instant and for eternity. Every loss, every hurt, every violence against you, even the most unimaginable thing that has happened to you will be restored—and you will be paid back one hundred fold. All with just a look at His face.

Ian: I know the answer to this because we have talked, but do you see everything I do?

Valor: [Laughs for a while.] It is so funny that you guys are so concerned about all that. We never invade your privacy or your intimacy.

This chat with Valor lasted about 60 minutes. During it, I was undone at various times. The understanding of how the Father speaks of us and brags about us completely wrecked me. The presence of God was so tangible I felt like I was in a different place. It felt surreal.

My simple point is that working with the angelic,

activating the angelic, and knowing we are doing this with help from the angelic is vital for all those who are on Kingdom mission. I believe we can all learn to see at some level. God uses our senses to let us feel heaven—and whether through taste, touch, sight, sound, or smell, we can learn to interpret what God is doing through the angelic in our midst. The doorway into growth is to lose judgment; when we see a fault in someone else, it usually means the same fault lies in us, only in a greater measure. It's the spot in someone else's eye versus the plank in our own (Matthew 7:3). Shunning judgment, even under the guise of discernment, is the gateway to growth in revelation.

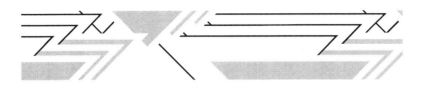

4

Kingdom Generosity

Hans Rosling is a Swedish doctor and statistician who specializes in global health statistics and has developed a method of presenting changes within nations in the last two centuries. What does he use to measure the development of global progress? Health and wealth.

Many are in complete opposition to the wealth and health message often promoted by preachers, some of whom are indeed scandalous. And let me be clear, a charlatan is a charlatan. Whether it's selling indulgences to the guilty or blessed water from Chernobyl, people claiming to represent Christ have used people's needs to get rich. It isn't only restricted only to those claiming to represent Christ though. Tales of New Age charlatans abound. Shamans, gurus, and psychics have all prospered through manipulation of the tormented.

I fully get it. But what I don't get is throwing out the baby with the bathwater.

The purpose of a counterfeit is to be seen as the real thing, not to be the best counterfeit around. Once a counterfeit is seen as a counterfeit, it is of zero value. I want to suggest that the existence of these charlatans does in fact point to something very real and very godly. There are heavenly principles of wealth that should not be ignored.

I find it fascinating that some people (sometimes I think it's the majority) have preached against the health and wealth gospel, while eating healthy foods, exercising, not going into debt, and saving money. One person I know—a preacher of great stature and a man of great faith—specifically lambasts the wealth doctrine. Meanwhile he has amassed a personal fortune in the millions. He has not sold snake oil, but he has bought properties, invested wisely, and received a handsome income from his large church. Not too much, just enough to be a good, middle-class guy. He doesn't drive a flashy car, not because he doesn't like them, but because—in his own words of wisdom to me—it would cause people in his congregation to judge him and to despise his wealth. So he keeps his personal fortune hidden from people. At least, he thinks he does, but really he doesn't. Most people know he is wealthy and has enough for a few more lifetimes if he needed it. They all collude with a system that allows us to preach against wealth while amassing a personal fortune that is private and no one's business.

Often the middle-class church and its leaders despise the wealth gospel, stating it is a sham that preys on the weak and needy. They tell their congregants not to get into debt, to get a job or a better job, and to work as hard as they can so they can save. It sounds like good stuff for the most part. I hate it though. It is probably one of the most selfish ways of thinking to be taught from the pulpit. "Have enough to give, to tithe, and to not be in debt. Manage your desires and only buy what you can afford" are really good pieces of advice to get free from financial bondage, but this is *not* the gospel's view of finances. This mindset of "just having enough" is the daily provision promised by God, not the abundance we need to change nations.

I tell my people that every single Christian should have a desire to be a multimillionaire. Yes, you have read that correctly. Every single Christian should desire to be a multimillionaire or even billionaire—not for our own personal gain, but to advance the Kingdom of God and fulfill His purposes.

Middle class ambivalence toward wealth is killing the proclamation of the gospel. We are to be content, not indifferent. I love my cars; I currently own a 1997 Jeep Wrangler (19 years old at the time of writing) and a 2006 Pontiac Solstice (10 years old at the time of writing). They are fun, reliable, don't cost me much, and I am so thankful for them. I would love a great car, but that thought doesn't get me out of bed in the morning. My wife and I live in a modest 1,200-square-foot house in a great area where we love our neighbors and love the neighborhood. It is cramped with five of us living there and only one bathroom. Of course it would be great to have a bigger house—but again, it's not what gets me out of bed each morning.

What motivates me is the proclamation and demonstration of the gospel of the Kingdom. I want to have millions of dollars to see churches planted, the homeless reached, poverty eradicated, healing rooms opened, art studios opened, and apostolic schools established that will train and mobilize five-fold ministers to cities and nations. I want to see widows and orphans taken care of and nations discipled. That will require many, many billions of dollars. And I may upgrade my house and car along the way.

Many church leaders I know criticize the wealth and abundance message while personally seeking to be wealthy, all set aside for a rainy day. They even hide their personal wealth from their congregations by driving modest cars and living in modest homes. I do not believe that anyone should save for retirement. God's plan is that old men and women will dream dreams, not plan on retiring. Save for your dreams—dreams of seeing this world become the Kingdom of our Lord and of His Christ—not of playing golf every day in Florida. Save for not being a burden on your children and grandchildren; save for a future and a hope—not a prolonged death plan!

Somehow we pat ourselves on the back for our good stewardship and management of our resources, believing it's the way we handle our finances that has made us wealthy. Let me explain wealthy. As of the end of 2015, if you personally earn $32,000 per year, you are in the top 1% of wealth globally. That doesn't include savings, just income. Even reaching the poverty line in the USA of just over $11,000 per year places you in the world's top 13%. We are wealthy, and by patting ourselves on the back, gesturing at giving thanks to God for what we have, sponsoring a child in Africa, and helping out a homeless person every now and again, the world turns. This is in direct alignment with the warning God gave us in Deuteronomy chapter 8. It tells us that the Kingdom blessings look like eating plenty, having more than enough resources, building nice houses, and our wealth multiplying—but we run the risk of believing this wealth comes from our own principles and not *the* principle that it is the Lord who gives us the power, strength, and ability to be wealthy. Wealth comes from Him and is intended to increase.

Jesus tells us that the enemy comes to steal, kill, and destroy but that Jesus came to give us life and an abundant life. The word "abundant" means more than enough. When we say, "I have enough" it is pure selfishness. Wealth isn't about you having enough; it's about you having more than enough so you can take care of the widows and the orphans and disciple nations.

I once took a friend of mine to the city of Chicago. He is someone who has rejected the wealth message while earning six figures in his church, investing in property and stocks, and traveling around the country selling his products and prophesying over leaders. Other than his rejection of the wealth message while personally gaining wealth, I have no problem with any of what he does or how he provides for his family. In fact, I love it. I took him to see the landmarks of the city and asked him how much he thought it cost to build the Trump Tower in Chicago. It cost just short of $900 million. How do we reach people that pay $1000 per night to stay in a hotel room and who spend $30 on a bottle of luxury "Bling" water? To reach people, we need money, and while we would all love to think this money will come from the sky in a miracle, chances are we need to embrace our role on this planet. If the wealth of Babylon is to be transferred to the Kingdom, it stands to reason that it will happen when people start discipling billionaires—not to selfishly get their hands on the wealthy's tithes, but to teach the church how to become wealthy.

I believe the church has abandoned cities throughout the world for a number of reasons. One of them is that it is just too expensive. In 2016, A third of an acre of land on Chicago's impoverished south side was listed for sale at $1.7 million, just for the land. A typical Chicago lot (130 feet by 25 feet) sells for a mere $1 million in wealthy River North. Meanwhile some 30 miles west in Carol Stream, a good solid suburb, you can buy three acres for $470,000 or 4.5 acres for $1.5 million. A lack of money is keeping us out of the cities. I know of two churches that are moving from the city to the neighboring suburbs simply because of the cost of property.

In my experience, Christians in the USA are the most generous people on earth. They give toward needs and they respond over and above when blessing pastors and fellow Christians. I just want them to have more to give.

So how do we become wealthy? The first step is to want it and want it badly. Check your heart here because it's not about the car you will drive or the properties you will own; it is about the impact you will make for the Kingdom. Next comes dispelling some great lies about wealth and poverty. Most of us have received the values of our parents about money. Just because we believe them, doesn't make them true!

Money Myths

Myth #1: I have worked hard for it, therefore it is mine to steward, and the best way of doing that is investing.

Stewardship has never been about saving. It is about using the resources given, resources that actually belong to someone else (God) for the appropriate purpose. Maybe you have been told your inheritance is for your family's future generations, but let me ask you this: What are they going to do with it? What they typically do with it is live a decent lifestyle, impact a few people, and try not to leave it in a worse state than they found it. Doesn't that remind you of the one who buried it away in the parable of the talents? Discover what

God wants you to do with your resources because even if it came from your great aunt Agnes who owned gold mines in Australia, it was never hers—it was always God's. Find out God's vision for what He has entrusted to you. The wealth of God is not supposed to bring you sorrow. Make it joyful. Find out God's heart for your wealth and invest it in those things. Invest in true riches of lives transformed and nations discipled. By all means, invest to create wealth, but create wealth for His purpose for your life.

Myth #2: God loves the poor and has a special place for them in His heart.

Of course God loves the poor, and the early church was certainly told not to forget them. They weren't told to make them their number one priority, but they were told not to forget them. I don't believe this meant to "go tell the poor it will be okay in heaven." What if remembering the poor meant to feed them, house them, clothe them, and give them a way out of poverty? You know what that takes—money. If you have ever been involved in grassroots social justice, you will know there isn't enough coming from the government in volume to solve the problem. It requires the church to be wealthy and mission focused.

Myth #3: Money won't make you happy.

Do you know what else won't make you happy? Being poor! For every Christian that glorifies poverty, I would like to show them what poverty looks like and take them on a tour of the West Side or South Side of

Chicago. For most of my life, I worked in the inner city. Do you know what poverty brings? Death and destruction. In Chicago it brings single parenting, poor housing, racism, drugs, gangs, murders, bad education, violence, early death, homelessness, and hopelessness, just to name a few. There is nothing, and I mean nothing, good about being poor or seeing a city or region ravished by poverty. Slums are not the creation of wealth. The burden of violence in Northern Ireland was on the shoulders of the poor while the wealthy were barely affected. Don't get me wrong. I am smart enough to know the cure is not simply giving people money, but let's not romanticize being poor. Working three jobs while trying to raise three kids was so hard on my mom that it's probably what ended up almost killing her until Jesus healed her.

Myth #4: Money is the root of all evil.

The scripture 1 Timothy 6:10 does not say money is the root of all evil, it says, "the love of money." Neither does it say "all evil," it says, "all kinds of evil." Paul makes it clear that his warning is based on the "foolish and harmful desires" and that it is not the inherent evil of money, but of the heart condition of one who is seduced by it. The person Paul is talking about is the one who gains wealth for his own pleasure, and that is not what I promote. I promote the desire to use wealth for the Kingdom. The vision needs to be for us to steward what God gives us for the sake of His Great Commission.

Without money, the Good Samaritan in Jesus' parable would simply have been a well-intentioned Samaritan! It was the access to finances that allowed him to meet the needs of a beaten-down, injured human being, set him back on his feet, and restore him. Do you know what else is at the root of a lot of evil? The love of poverty. How will being poor rescue widows and orphans?

Myth #5: God will meet your needs but not your wants.

I thank God that He meets my needs. I have testimony after testimony of how God has shown up to meet unexpected and often sudden needs. Certainly Scripture talks about seeking first the Kingdom and "all these things will be added" (Matthew 6:33). What are these things? Food and clothing and provision from God to name a few. Scripture also guarantees us that when "The Lord is my shepherd I shall not want" (Psalm 23:1). The word "want" means want or lack. In other words, there should be no lack when Jesus is your shepherd. No lack for doing what He has commissioned us to do.

Myth #6: God does not like rich people. He loves everyone, but doesn't really like rich people.

The Rich Young Ruler

And someone came to Him and said, "Teacher, what good thing shall I do that I may obtain eternal life?" And He said to him, "Why are you asking Me about what is good? There is only One who is good; but if you wish to enter into life, keep the commandments." Then he said to Him, "Which ones?" And Jesus said, "You shall not commit murder; You shall not commit adultery; You shall not steal; You shall not bear false witness; Honor your father and mother; and You shall love your neighbor as yourself." The young man said to Him, "All these things I have kept; what am I still lacking?" Jesus said to him, "If you wish to be complete, go and sell your possessions and give to the poor, and you will have treasure in Heaven; and come, follow Me." But when the young man heard this statement, he went away grieving; for he was one who owned much property.

And Jesus said to His disciples, "Truly I say to you, it is hard for a rich man to enter the Kingdom of Heaven. Again I say to you, it is easier for a camel to go through the eye of a needle, than for a rich man to enter the Kingdom of God" (Matthew 19:16–24).

I am going to guess that you have not personally done what Jesus required in this scripture. That means you either don't believe it, you live in guilt, you only think it's for people richer than you, or that maybe Jesus is not saying being wealthy is bad but that your attitude toward wealth is important. Maybe there are more options, but most of us believe Jesus is getting to the heart of the rich, young ruler, not just his bank account. We believe He is saying that if there is anything more important to us than Jesus, then we should get rid of it.

I also want to suggest there is a subtle message embraced by a lot of Christians, which is it's not good to be wealthy. That's baloney. God does not like it when *anything* takes His place in our lives, but He outrageously loves everyone, rich and poor. Your wealth status has nothing to do with how God feels about you. It has probably more to do with how you feel about you!

I teach my kids and our church that there are four things we can do with our money: tithe, give, save, and spend.

Tithe

I do not believe that Old Testament tithing is applicable under the New Covenant. I used to, but I don't anymore. I teach giving to the church as the first thing we do, and that everyone should do, and that 10% is a good starting point but a lousy finishing point. We want to grow in every area of our lives (at least I hope we do). If I give 10% when I get saved, and I am still giving 10% years later, my giving has not grown. Sure, the amount may have grown through promotions and better wages, but the percent has not changed. I don't give to avoid a curse; I do it to receive a blessing. The blessing is being part of something greater than I am, playing a role in the life of a local church, and owning the vision of the church. I believe the tithe should go to the local church and should be regular and consistent—and then we get to give more to the things God has placed on our hearts.

I have witnessed people becoming more excited about the church when they first start giving. Some wait until they feel something before giving, but it works the other way around as well. Our hearts will align with where we place our treasure (Luke 12:34). I can often tell when someone is about to leave the church as they normally stop giving a few months before they leave. Once they stop giving, the disconnect between them and the local church grows and becomes final. I don't think I have ever seen someone stop giving, resolve their issues with the church, and begin giving again. It is an absolute indication of the individual's heart for the church. Consumers, those who come to receive and not build, are often the worst givers. The connection between the heart and wallet is very strong: if you want your heart to change, then give.

Can you imagine sitting on a plane, bus, or train and reading the book of the person who is in front of or beside you? Can you imagine asking him or her not to turn the page because you haven't finished reading it? Asking that person to hold the page while you go to the bathroom? To bookmark the page so you can pick up tomorrow where you left off? What about the refrigerator in the breakroom at work? What if you had brought in some Giordano's pizza for lunch, and when you went to eat it, you saw someone had taken a slice? What if someone uses your home WiFi from across the street? We would accept none of these as being okay, yet we come to church, utilize the programs, enjoy the heating and air conditioning, the worship instruments, the audio-visual equipment, and enjoy the ministry of the pastor—and we expect to get it for free, thinking someone else can pay for it. Or we think we can't afford to tithe. The problem is not in your bank account; it is in your heart.

Give

Giving to missions, missionaries, and good causes should all be in addition to what you give to the local church. I also believe you should give to individuals, especially church leaders. First, Paul tells Timothy that elders, especially those who labor in preaching and doctrine, are worthy of double honor. That word "honor" has its root in payment or monetary reward. Second, one of the most often misquoted verses in the New Testament is quoted as "my God shall supply all **my** needs according to His riches in Glory" (author's emphasis). But the Bible doesn't say that. The text in Philippians is a blessing from an apostle over people who reached into their pockets and gave to him financially to the point where he had an abundance. Paul said: "And **my** God will supply all **your** needs according to His riches in glory in Christ Jesus" (Philippians 4:19). Paul was telling them that he was not seeking the gift but the profit it brings to their account. Understand this: by sowing into Paul, those who did it profited from it, and Paul was convinced that his God would provide for their needs, not according to the riches of this earth but the riches of God Himself. They financially blessed Paul, they profited directly because of this, and God measured this profit according to His riches. I do not believe this is speaking of only financial profit, although I do believe that is part of it. I believe it refers to the riches of heaven, of destiny, purpose, and the expansion of the Kingdom in the life of the giver.

Save

Yes, we should save, and we should do it with purpose. For most of us, saving will be to fulfill our dreams and desires as we grow old. These dreams and desires should be rooted in the Kingdom of God, not the acquisition of stuff.

Spend

Of course we should spend money. My family shops in cheap grocery stores, have old cars that are a lot of fun but cost us little, and we eat out a lot. Using our money this way buys us time. I actually think this is one of the most useful things money does—buy time. It costs more for a direct flight, but it buys you time. Money also buys you energy. A good hotel costs more than a cheap motel, but it buys you rest and a good night's sleep, and maybe even some extra services that allow you to rest and replenish. Having someone clean your house buys you both time and energy. It's the same with a personal chef—you buy time, energy, and health.

I had a computer for nine years. It was so old that it

would take about 30 minutes to start up. I preach from my computer, so I would have to get it started before I got up to preach. I don't know how much time I wasted on that thing, but it was a lot. I replaced everything I could, including the hard drive, power supply, and memory, and it helped for a while but it was just old. It was this notion of actually spending money to buy time that convinced me it was okay to get a new computer. As the church buys it for me, I wanted to make sure I was handling this resource as a good steward. And then my wife pointed out that I was not stewarding what was even more important—my time.

The same is true of ministers who buy jets. I am sure there are some who like the ego boost, but all the ones I know do it because they were wasting so much time missing planes, getting delayed, and catching connecting flights that are frequently cancelled or delayed. That is a waste of a very finite resource—time. I have a dear friend whose health has suffered because she travels so much. She is one of the most truly humble and gifted people I know. She travels almost every week, often out of her own pocket, to poor churches who cannot afford to fly her in. So she buys cheap flights, sits in coach, flies at very awkward times, and her sleep pattern is so wrecked and her back is so sore that she is operating purely on the grace and mercy of God. If I could, I would buy her a plane and two pilots so she would be able to sleep, be refreshed, and minister for many more years.

Money simply allows you to say yes and those "yeses" should bring life and freedom and enhance your family. Abundance goes way deeper than mere money. We all know people who are wealthy and who are not happy. They are not living from a place of wealth. Being wealthy is, like everything else, an inside job. I can have an abundant mindset with zero in my bank account, and I can have a poverty mindset with millions of dollars in my bank account. The goal is abundance, and I believe when we talk about money, when we preach and teach about money, we often do it from a poverty mindset. We tend to hide our wealth, be ashamed of it, become afraid others will judge us based on what we do or do not have—and then we end up teaching from a place of lack instead of abundant provision.

God wants you to be wealthy, to build houses and live in them, to have your business grow and prosper, and for everything you have to prosper. One of the great declarations over the people of God was "there will be no poor among you." We must get rid of the poverty mindset that amasses private wealth for ourselves—and create Kingdom wealth for the sake of a hurting world.

However, there will be no poor among you, since the Lord will surely bless you in the land which the Lord your God is giving you as an inheritance to possess, if only you listen obediently to the voice of the Lord your God, to observe carefully all this commandment which I am commanding you today. For the Lord your God will bless you as He has promised you, and you will lend to many nations, but you will not borrow; and you will rule over many nations, but they will not rule over you (Deuteronomy 14:4-6).

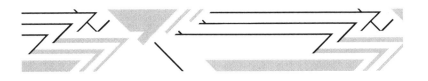

5

Honor

Read and listen to everything by Danny Silk. That could be the end of this chapter. Really, Danny is a genius and has managed to distill teaching on honor in very real, connected, and helpful ways. I do not really want to repeat what Danny teaches, so I will tell you how we have implemented a culture of honor and some of the lessons we have learned along the way. I am fairly certain all of this comes from Danny. Even the lessons we learned were often from reaching out to him and getting advice from him. Visit www.lovingonpurpose.com for more info on Danny.

As mentioned earlier, this journey of Greater Chicago Church really started in 2008 at a School of Supernatural Strategic Planning led by Paul Manwaring. I took some of our staff and church board to Redding and for five days we sat in a classroom trying to work out our next steps. As a result of that meeting, we invited Paul and his wonderful wife Sue to come and teach a conference on *A Culture of Honor*. We were enamored by Bethel's culture and wanted what they had. I was once in a meeting with other leaders when a pastor asked Danny Silk about the culture of honor, and the pastor (poor guy) said he loved the idea of this culture coming to his church because his people would finally honor him. It was kind of awkward because most of us knew this was the wrong perspective, but I also suspect that most of us also secretly wanted what this man had expressed.

It has certainly been true of not only pastors, but congregants who—when they hear of the culture of honor, feel that at last they will get the respect they need or deserve. Our journey with honor has been far from smooth. We have learned many things—which really means we have made many mistakes—and continue to learn and implement this culture. This is some of that story. At its finest, the culture of honor is about valuing everyone from heaven's eyes, not earth's. We see the gold in everyone, looking for that piece of people that points to their identity as a child of God. It empowers, brings freedom, replaces fear with love, and doesn't seek to punish people. In fact, being unpunishable is core to this culture.

Changing our culture

You will never, and I mean never, create an atmosphere or culture around you that isn't in you. You can always tell what really goes on with a leader by the people they reproduce. My three kids share my physical DNA, and my spiritual kids share my spiritual DNA. They are not my clones; they are my offspring. That means the first thing a leader of a church or organization must change is his or her personal culture before it will affect the culture around them. This takes time, patience, and growth. Growth simply means you won't have it all sorted and will make mistakes, and these mistakes will affect the people you lead. Vulnerability and transparency, along with a good dose of courage and security, will be needed on the journey.

I read everything I could about honor—from the honor code of the military, the honor code of the McCoys and the Hatfields, the honor code of the Mafia, and to everything Danny Silk wrote or spoke about. At great cost, I attended every School of Transformation Bethel ran. I started building relationships with other pastors that had adopted this change, talked with them frequently, asked them a lot of questions, and brought them into our church at every opportunity. When changing things personally and corporately, nothing beats hunger!

Honor and sonship are how we disciple people. It's learning and changing from the inside. Honor is not something we do; it is who we are. This is an internal alignment with heaven that affects what we do, but it is first and foremost becoming more like Jesus.

When we first started teaching this, we used to say that the first rule of honor was that we don't get to control others, we only get to control ourselves. This is really important. I do not allow your bad behavior to stop me from being the best version of me. Sadly, what many people heard, particularly people who don't do authority and relationships well, or those who resist change because they are so hurt from past experiences (real experiences of being hurt by the church or others around them) was "No one gets to control me!" That resulted in some very unhelpful outcomes. The moment their boss told them to do something they didn't like, they felt controlled. The moment a church leader asked them to do something in a certain way, or confronted them if something they were responsible for was not done at all, they felt controlled. We started to hear people say, "I don't feel very honored right now." Of course I want everyone to feel honored, but something felt a little off with that statement. After a while, I came to the conclusion that saying this was a fundamental flaw in our understanding of honor. It was defining honor more like a trait that required everyone else to change while I remained the same. It was influenced by "fundamental attribution error." This is the tendency we have to see and experience someone's behavior or actions and attribute an internal cause for them, while not actually knowing (or even while ignoring) any external factors, and at the same time, understanding these situational factors have influenced our own behavior and are therefore justifiable when it comes to us.

For example, if you and I both take a driving test and we both fail, I might think you are a bad driver and didn't put effort into the test, but think I'm a good driver who had an instructor who was really hard to please. After digging into the material Danny has made, I realized that *honor is never expected, it is only given.* That shifted so many things. It allowed us to seek to understand the actions of another, and even if we did not agree with someone's conclusions, it helped us have a degree of empathic understanding of the other person. Always show up wearing love as a blanket. This has become our first law of honor.

Colossians 3:14 The Amplified Bible: "*Beyond all these things put on and wrap yourselves in [unselfish] love*"

Colossians 3:14 The Message: "*So, chosen by God for this new life of love, dress in the wardrobe God picked out for you: compassion, kindness, humility, quiet strength, discipline"*

Around the same time, we had people, mostly leaders, who would respond to the "I don't feel honored" statement by using what we had learned as a weapon—a way of building a wall against another. They would respond with "I don't get to control you or your feelings, I can only control me and I am good." Again, this sounded completely congruent with what we had learned about only being able to control ourselves. One of my staff at the time even suggested with great frequency that anyone who came to confront him about something should get some inner healing or deliverance. After all, he didn't get to control the other person so they were the ones who needed to adjust. I am sure it was from a pastoral heart! Back to the teachings I went—and concluded that we had the boundary in place (the boundary between what I have the power to control and what you have the power to control) but we were missing a piece about connection. The goal in all of these conversations, particularly vital in confrontation, was to increase connection. Under the guise of not controlling another or being responsible for their feelings, we were creating distance and disconnect. We have found that using connecting statements and questions has been really important. "How can I help?" and "What do you need from me?" have been really helpful. Even more helpful is when we start caring about the other person—not getting anxious about being right or wrong or about getting punished, but simply doing all we can to understand. We try to understand the internal and external circumstances that have brought people to where they are. And thus we came across another pitfall.

The real goal in understanding is to try to build intimacy with the other person. We apparently don't do that by diagnosing them! We have lots of very discerning people in our church and in our leadership, and the risk is that we start telling people the truth we have about them. But intimacy is not built by telling other people what you believe is the truth about them; intimacy is built when you tell them the truth about what is going on with you. I think this is almost a direct quote from Danny—and one truth that is so hard to do! The church, especially one focused on transformation, often sees it's role as being to diagnose and treat. Instead, the real transformation happens when we love, connect, and care.

We have learned that building connections is crucial in a culture of honor. I used to rock climb. I was never very good, but I was enthusiastic. There are two ways to climb (I am ignoring the option to free climb): either by top roping or by placing protection. In top roping, someone takes their place at the top of a climb, usually just by hiking to the top of the cliff. They secure themselves, and then they drop a rope to the climber at the bottom. That climber secures the rope to his or her harness and when both people are ready, they start to climb. The person at the top continually takes in the slack of the rope so if the climber falls, they will not fall far. The other way to climb is for one of the climbers to secure himself to the bottom of the climb with one end of the rope, and the other to fasten his or her rope to their harness. Again, the person securing the climber takes in the slack—but instead of taking up slack, they the rope is let out as the climber ascends. While ascending, the climber places protection into nooks and crannies in the rock and runs the rope through the protection. If the climber falls with this method, he will fall twice the distance between himself and the last piece of protection. Some climbs are difficult enough that people use two ropes. The protection is everything. After that comes the strength of the rope. Hopefully I have communicated this well enough to give a picture of what happens.

In the culture of honor, we have some protection and we have a rope. The rope is the trust built between people. I don't believe trust is ever earned. Scripture tells me that love always trusts (1 Corinthians 13:7), so it is therefore something I give people. If I am dependent on you doing things to get something from me, that can become a codependent mess very quickly. The same goes for anger. You don't make me angry; I choose to be angry. If I need you to do something to make me less angry, then you are in charge of my emotions. In this scenario, if you don't do something, I have a reason to not change, to not forgive, to not build connection. However, I am responsible for creating the right conditions and making it as easy as possible for you to trust me. I will never be able to do that if connection is not important to me. The rope of trust starts off fairly flimsy, more like a thread than a rope. If something comes up, if I behave in a way that is scary, the thread is easily broken. No one uses thread to climb. Some people climb alone, trusting only themselves, but it is a lonely adventure that often ends in death or injury. As we build shared experiences, as we learn about each other and know that we care for each other, the rope eventually forms into a thick rope capable of withstanding multiple long falls on the trickiest routes. After long falls, the rope must be replaced, but it is never replaced by a thread. It starts at the thickness it was when we left off. Trust, built by a commitment to connect, is the rope of our adventures together. When one party doesn't want to climb any more, there is nothing you can do except keep the rope at hand, ready to pick up where you left off.

This becomes especially true for church leaders. I

have wondered why churches are often so resistant to change. I know of one church that blew up over what to do with the discretionary spending decisions in their annual budget. The board had a couple of very successful and very wealthy men on it. These men met every week to discuss the discretionary spend. It was a small church with a healthy income and large costs. Do you know how much the discretionary spend was? It was $1000 a year. Three successful, wealthy men were meeting once a week to go over plans to spend $20 a week. The children's ministry would ask for things that weren't in their budget, and these men would see it as their God-given stewardship responsibility to pray about this and make a decision about buying Sharpies or glitter versus a new kettle for the kitchen. Change seemed impossible for this church, and I believe that both the continual discussion of how to spend $20 a week and their being reluctant to change stemmed from the absence of trust and connection.

Pastors who intuitively know there is an absence of trust and connection understand that they won't be able to change their churches. "My church isn't ready for that" is code for there not being enough trust, and "My people would never permit the organ to be replaced by a keyboard" tells me there has not been enough relational trust built. So churches stay the same, satisfied with trust being like a thread, incapable of pulling someone up a rock face.

The protections we have come in all shapes and sizes. Climbers use wedges, chocks, and cams. We use the five-fold ministry, covenant, an abundant mindset, and conflict. Yes, you read it right, conflict. I would suggest you read Danny's book *Culture of Honor* or watch his fabulous video series at his Loving on Purpose Life Academy for more information direct from the source, but I will give you my take on the practice and implementation of these protections. Like in climbing, they are only useful if you use them well.

The Five-fold

When Scripture talks about Jesus' ascension, it means He took up His seat by the Father and ruled the earth. The truth that Jesus is King means we are not waiting for something else to happen for Him to be King: He is King. When Ephesians 4 talks about Jesus ascending, taking His rightful place as King, it is interesting that what He does as part of His role as King is establish His government on earth by giving apostles, prophets, evangelists, pastors, and teachers. God's governmental authority on earth is what we call the five-fold. They are people, not job descriptions or abilities. In 1 Corinthians 12, we are told that God appointed gifts in the church, and the first gift was apostles. Coming first could mean they were the first to be appointed, they came before everyone else, or that there is a rank or order assigned by the Greek word used here for "first," which is *proton*. Apostles were indeed the first chronologically to be given to the church. They were also the first in order of rank in the New Testament church. I am not going to go into a long list of reasons why I believe the five-fold is still in operation. (There has been much written about it by people well more qualified than I am.) What I would like to approach is how we have found the implementation of the five-fold in our culture of honor.

One of the dangers when we start talking about this culture is that we tend to believe it means everyone is equal, and because honor is given to all men according to Peter (1 Peter 2:17), what results is some form of Christian Marxism. This culture is not leadership-less. In fact, in a culture of honor, the leader appointed by God is needed in a greater way. There is as a flow from heaven to earth and we must align ourselves with that flow. Alignment with an apostle is very important and so is keeping that alignment. It speaks to the principles of sonship and of submission. I do not want to labor these, but in a culture of honor, finding your apostle and making sure your values and priorities are aligned with him or her provides a protection from simply doing your own thing.

This relationship is managed from our end—each persons end—not from the apostle's end. Therein lies the difference between this and other forms of church culture. If I say Bill Johnson is my apostle, what is important to him becomes important to me. Bill tells a story about a man petting a dog. Someone came up to the man and told him he was petting the dog the wrong way, going against the fur. The man's response was that the dog should move. My job, in alignment with Bill, is to understand that it is not Bill changing to meet my values that will cause heaven to break out, rather it is my choice to shift my position to align with him. I have been told I am an apostle—and while it has taken me a while to embrace this, and truthfully, just get over myself, I still need to be in alignment with someone who I consider a global apostle. It does not mean that Bill even knows who I am, but it does mean that I make my priorities come into alignment with his priorities.

When we left the Vineyard Association, it was based on alignment. I was approached by a leader in the Vineyard who asked me the insightful question, "Who is your Daddy?" All the guest speakers we had were from Bethel. I was pursuing relationships with people from Bethel and chose to attend Bethel's conferences, including their leadership conferences, over attending the Vineyard ones. I am sure some of it was a little rebellious, but in my heart of hearts, I believed I was pursuing the mandate of the Vineyard by going after "the best" and running with it. The problem was that I was misaligned. So, after some soul-searching and much prayer, we decided to fully align with Bethel. We don't call ourselves Bethel, but we have embraced the teaching and practice of Bethel church.

Heaven has order. God's government on earth has order. That order is first apostles, and we lead from there.

Covenant

None of this works without covenant. In a nutshell, covenant is about making a lifelong commitment to stay in relationship, bolting the back door so leaving because we are hurt is not an option, and lifting each other up, believing the best about each other, and remaining unoffendable. There is a book in each one of these statements. Covenant is never tested when we all agree and everything is wonderful. It is tested when someone does something that you think you will never recover from. To use a phrase from Danny Silk, it is saying that I will take a bullet for you, even it is from you.

You don't withdraw a covenant with another, you rip it up. Most of us know the one real covenant is to your spouse and we also know people who have broken that covenant. Breaking a covenant of any form is painful for both parties. It is a serious business to make a covenant and should not be taken lightly.

An Abundant Mindset

Simply put, there is enough anointing, favor, promotion, money, status, and power for everyone. An abundant mindset is at war with orphan thinking and is necessary to avoid much of the striving and competition that exists in the church.

An abundant mindset allows me to rejoice when someone is better at something than I am, and it often means I am about to get an upgrade! Begrudgery, resentment, and envy are marginalized with this mindset. You don't have to fight, cajole, and manipulate to get something—because with an abundant mindset, you know that what is coming to you will come regardless of what goes to others.

Conflict

I am in relationship with a number of churches that have asked me to come and help them with their culture. As I share how amazing my leaders are and how we have this amazing culture, it is easy to hear that we float on clouds and dance along the streets with birds on our shoulders. This book I've written is so important to my leaders and me simply because we have fought together, and at times with each other, over these values. I tell people that we have killed for them. We haven't literally killed of course, but we have killed some mindsets and belief systems that continually try to override our culture. This is why conflict is so important. Oftentimes church leaders deal with conflict by being afraid of it or by doing everything in their power to avoid it. Our experience of conflict is normally negative, so shifting our perspective to seeing conflict as a good thing can be really challenging. When conflict arises, the sky is not falling, God is still good, and you may not be perfect, but that is okay. Don't be afraid; His plans and promises are still at work.

Here are some things I have learned about conflict:

- Fear is the enemy of all healthy conflict. Keep your love on. I read a good book about that and you should too. (If you don't know what I'm referring to, it's Danny Silk's book *Keep Your Love On*.)

- If someone has decided to disconnect, nothing you do or don't do will be good enough. Successful conflict requires covenant and connection, or at least a burning desire to increase connection. If that only exists with one party, the conflict will probably not be resolved.

- Conflict presents as behaviors, decisions, and even sins, but these are seldom the real issue. Knowing what the problem really is before you try solving it is well worth the effort spent trying to get to the bottom of it. "What is the problem we are trying to resolve?" is *the* question. There may be times when there is little you can do to solve the problem unless everyone involved recognizes it and wants to make necessary changes.

- When I make stuff up about what you are doing, thinking, and feeling, that is not truth. Truth is when I show you what is going on inside of me and essentially asking, "Does this matter to you? Do you care?" At times I have been told that it doesn't matter, the person doesn't care, and they have walked out and told people I was uncaring. When this happens, I get to be a Christian and walk in forgiveness, blessing, and honor. What a privilege!

- Conflict is not about being right or wrong; it is about understanding and connection. If those aren't reciprocated, keep your love on, believe the best about the other person, and make a way for them to rejoin you when that changes.

- Forgive and learn to ask for forgiveness. "I am sorry you were hurt by thinking I said _____" is not the same as saying, "I am sorry I hurt you." The latter enters into the other person's world and experiences and expresses true empathy, while the former shifts blame. Empathy works.

- Every time you experience conflict, you get better at it. Every victory you win for the heart of someone else establishes you as a warrior in the Kingdom. This is sometimes the greatest battle we have.

After sonship, nothing has changed us as a church more than honor. Honor can create a ceiling for the miraculous. Remember that Jesus could only do a few miracles in His hometown due to the lack of honor (Mark 6:4–5). Creating a culture of honor is also a journey. Get help from people who have walked the journey longer than you. Read their books, listen to their teachings, and get yourself radically transformed.

6

The Advancing Kingdom

When I was 16 years old, I was asked to teach at my church. It was a house church and I was the youngest there at the time. The leader, a man I am indebted to for so much, must have recognized something in me and asked me to "share from the Word" at the Friday night Bible study. I picked the only passage familiar to me. I had only been saved a few months and knew very little about the Bible. Armed with my *Strong's Bible* and *Vine's Greek Dictionary*, I began looking at the Lord's Prayer. That Friday I spoke for what seemed like an eternity, but it actually only about 20 minutes. I shared everything I had prepared during the week. I even took a day off school just to prepare.

When I mentioned "Thy Kingdom come, on earth as it is in heaven" (Matthew 6:10), in my naiveté I told everyone that Jesus must have wanted His rule and reign on earth now. Otherwise why would He pray for it? If He wanted us to pray for His return, surely He would have asked us to do that. Heaven on earth. That's what He prayed. Afterwards I was taken aside and was very gently, very lovingly told "We don't believe that here."

It turns out what "we" believed was that God's experiment with the nation of Israel failed or stalled, so God made Plan B and called it the Church. He had not finished with Israel, but for now He was in the business of saving people from every tribe and tongue until He got angry enough to secretly return and rapture The Church. Then He would finish His business with Israel, finally return for real this time, and establish His Kingdom on earth as it is in heaven. Of course if you have read the Word, that makes most of the New Testament irrelevant to us today. If the Kingdom is yet to come, we must disregard all parables mentioning the Kingdom, throw out Jesus' proclamation about the Kingdom growing, and consider John the Baptist crazy for preaching that the Kingdom is at hand. I sensed this "Kingdom stuff" was dangerous and could lead to theological debate, so I stayed away from it for years.

When I encountered the Holy Spirit seven years later, I was exposed to teachings from people who believed differently than I had been taught. We had been taught that Jesus was going to return to bring His Kingdom and our job was to evangelize until He returned. These new people talked about the Kingdom here on earth, and it was exciting to say the least. Of course, in pursuing the Kingdom, I prayed for people, saw demons cast out, and saw people healed, but it felt like there was a ceiling—not everyone was healed and not everyone was set free. Then I came across the teaching that stated the Kingdom is now, and also not yet. Yes, we are to pursue the Kingdom, but we had a reason for why some people were not healed: the Kingdom was delayed. When I first encountered this theology, it was like a breath of fresh air. Finally a lot of things made sense, and when practicing the Vineyard church's five-step healing model, we had a way to understand why people were not always healed. Many of my prayers would end in asking God to give people grace for their sickness. There was a huge flaw in this teaching: it produced a lot of faith for the "not yet" and much less for the "now" of the Kingdom. Like all good revelation, it was incredibly helpful for its time and caused many of us to get excited to see His Kingdom move on earth, but there is always development, learning, and fresh revelation.

When I first read Bill Johnson's book *When Heaven Invades Earth*, I would read a couple of pages, set it down, and pace around the room. It blew my mind. His focus was on expansion—the advancing of the Kingdom—not on blaming God for delaying something, playing a seemingly cruel game of dangling a carrot in front of us to keep us searching for the unobtainable.

The "now and not yet" theory is based on teachings from the 1950s by George Ladd. In a nutshell, it states that we live between the times. We live in "this present evil age" and during this time, the "age to come" breaks in and we get a taste of the Kingdom as it will be. As believers, we have free access to the age to come. As a framework for the miraculous in a dispensational theology, it worked for me for a long time. My mom was healed, I have been healed, and I have seen others healed, saved, and set free, all while believing the "now and the not yet." But I have shifted what I believe. I was never fully comfortable with the dispensational theology despite it being the norm for the church in which I was born again. I hated the idea of a delayed Kingdom and saw none of it in the New Testament. Of course, one could argue that a Kingdom praxis is still entirely workable in a "now and not yet" mindset, which is true, but if something is to be weighed by its fruit, the fruit of reinforcing delay is that we stop contending for the Kingdom. I also hated the idea of the rapture. I found it incongruent with the nature of God as I know Him, but my biggest issue with dispensationalism was making the rapture and/or the return of Jesus the central event in history. I believe that the birth, life, death, burial, resurrection, and ascension of Jesus the Messiah and the coming of His Spirit at Pentecost was and always will be the central event in all time and that the cross was *completely* sufficient for the New Covenant to be made and for the Kingdom to advance. I am not waiting for anything else to happen for the Kingdom to be manifest on earth as it is in heaven.

Paul understood that the Kingdom had come. He saw the resurrected Jesus and knew. He saw the Spirit poured out on all flesh and knew. The Old Testament is filled with the tension of waiting for the Kingdom, but there is none of this tension in the New Testament. Instead there are simply instructions for perseverance, faith, and contending for this Kingdom.

Our experience of not getting breakthrough, of not seeing everyone healed, or the power of the gospel not being demonstrated, cannot be neatly tied up by creating a theology where God is the One to blame. We are the Body of Christ here on earth and have been promised that we will do greater things and walk in all authority. I strongly believe that if we put as much effort into growing in authority, honor, sonship, generosity, working with the angelic, and being a prophetic voice that calls dry bones to live as we do in waiting for the "rapture bus" to come, we would be seeing more of His Kingdom on earth. That's why we contend for the Kingdom—to build in us the kind of atmosphere present in heaven and let it loose on the earth. God has nothing more to do, but we do.

Our church's mission is to transform and equip people to contend for the Kingdom of God. It is not to transform and equip them to deal with the "not yet." Our focus remains to see the Kingdom come and His will being done on earth as it is in heaven. We are contending for the now, not the "not yet." I tell our people they can believe whatever they want about the end times as long as it does not dilute a couple of scriptures.

There will be no end to the increase of His government or of peace (Isaiah 9:7).

But we all, with unveiled face, beholding as in a mirror the glory of the Lord, are being transformed into the same image from glory to glory, just as from the Lord, the Spirit (2 Corinthians 3:18).

As long as there is continual increase of His rule and reign, and as long as we are moving from glory to glory, believe what you want.

Ern Baxter, a leader in the Discipleship Movement of the 1970s, used to say any gospel of delay was a "bastard gospel." I think he is right if for no other reason than it produces more faith in the God of delay than the God of right now. It removes Jesus from His throne and places Him in a waiting room until He is actually crowned King. I don't require faith for delay; I do require faith for the right now.

Answering the question "Who is Jesus to you right now?" should elicit responses that include Savior and Lord. Those are wonderful, but Jesus is way more than that. He is in fact, right now as you read this, the King of the earth. We are not waiting on Him to get His crown, nor are we looking forward to Him taking His seat at the right hand of the Father where all authorities, angels, and powers are subject to Him (Acts 7:55–56; Romans 8:34; Ephesians 1:20; Colossians 3:1; Hebrews 1:3; Hebrews 8:1; Hebrews 10:12; Hebrews 12:2; 1 Peter 3:22; Revelation 3:21; Matthew 22:44; Acts 2:33). The cross defeated Satan once and for all.

There was a practice in Biblical times that when an enemy king was conquered, he would be paraded naked through the streets to demonstrate that he was defeated and ruled no more. This is how Eugene Petersen translates Colossians 2:15:

"He stripped all the spiritual tyrants in the universe of their sham authority at the Cross and marched them naked through the streets" (The Message).

The enemy has been defeated. The Kingdom is at hand, among us, and in us, and it's the Father's good pleasure to give us this Kingdom. The cross was the finished work of Jesus. We require nothing more—no works, no penance, and no indulgences. I am not waiting for anything else to happen that will finish what Jesus accomplished on the cross. The return of Jesus will not be about Him coming to rule and reign on earth; He has left us behind to do just that. Our mission, should we chose to accept it, is not to hunker down and wait until Jesus comes or calls: it is to enact the Kingdom He brought. The question should not be "Why isn't everyone healed?" The question should be "How do we walk in more healing and more authority to do what we are called to do?" If we spent as much time on answering this question as we do when we make charts, blogs, books, and bad movies, perhaps the kingdom of this world would look more like the Kingdom of our God and Jesus Christ.

I will spend my life pursuing the transformation and equipping of people to contend for this Kingdom. Some have said that because it is already given, we don't need to contend for it. I think this misses the point. Jesus did it all, but if I have issues with authority, I cannot walk in authority. If I have issues with believing I am loved and made in the image of God, I won't really believe I have significance to do anything. If I have issues with abundance and knowing whether or not I am worth anything, I will expect nothing. And so it goes. The contending is based on me being transformed into this Kingdom-bringer Jesus intended. If and when there is apparent delay, I need to contend. John Wimber, the founder of the Vineyard movement, asked God why he wasn't seeing more healings. He felt God tell him the problem wasn't on God's end. Any adjustment should come from our end and not from the fabrication of a theology that changes the character of God and gives us an excuse to not confront the problems of this world head-on. The Kingdom comes not by our might or our power but by His Spirit (Zechariah 4:6).

For those who say we don't need to do anything, in the words of Jerry Maguire, "Show me the money!" Show me the dead raised, the blind seeing, the deaf hearing, and I will listen. As for me, I will build contenders for the Kingdom.

In Matthew 16:19, Jesus tells Peter that he will be given the keys to the Kingdom. In Acts 2, a new, emboldened Peter took these keys and made them known for all to take hold of. Repent, get your sins forgiven, be baptized, and get filled with the Holy Spirit.

Repent

The Greek word for "repent" is *metanoeō* and you may find it might annoy you. *Metanoeō*—might annoy you. Get it? And moving swiftly on ... Most of us know by now that "repent" does not mean being sorry for your sins. According to Paul in 2 Corinthians 7, the sorrow that comes from the world causes death, but it is godly sorrow that leads us to repentance. Staying stuck in shame and sorrow for sins is an indication that no great repentance has actually taken place and that we have not changed how we think about our sins. The Holy Spirit does not convict you of your sins. How can He? If God has chosen to remember your sins no more, how can the Holy Spirit be any different? The role of the Holy Spirit is to convict you of your righteousness in Christ. His job is always to bring your focus back on Jesus, not yourself. John 16:8–11 tells us the Holy Spirit will convict the world concerning sin, righteousness, and judgment, and that He will convict us concerning righteousness and will remind everyone that Satan has been judged.

And He, when He comes, will convict the world concerning sin and righteousness and judgment; concerning sin, because they do not believe in Me; and concerning righteousness, because I go to the Father and you no longer see Me; and concerning judgment, because the ruler of this world has been judged (John 16:8–11).

To repent means to change our thinking. The word "repent" is almost always used in relation to sin, but we must change our thinking about our sins. I want to suggest that the mindset change necessary is to fully embrace our righteousness instead of our unrighteousness. We must reconsider our sins through the lens of the New Covenant, not the Old Covenant that has been rendered obsolete. Fully embrace that we have been made righteous, not by anything we have done or will do, but through the work of Jesus. Sin separated us from God, not Him from us. We were reconciled with Him, but He never left. In the garden, after Adam and Eve fell, God still showed up for their daily get-together. God does not tolerate our sinfulness, so He removed it through the sacrifice of Jesus on the cross.

I don't believe repentance is only about changing how we think about sin. I think it is a move away from an old pattern of scripts handed down from generation to generation and from our own learning through habits, success and failures. We tend to think from earth to heaven, and repentance calls us to do the opposite—think from heaven to earth. There must be a conscious leaving behind of old thinking. We are to reconsider how we think, leave the old behind, and discover what heaven is thinking about things.

Sins Forgiven and Be Baptized

I know I have already discussed this a bit, but it is absolutely vital for us to understand that the moment I place trust in something I can do to become righteous, that is self-righteousness. Baptism is a dramatic and prophetic account of what is actually taking place in the life of the new believer. He or she is entering the water complete with their "old flesh" and once they are submerged, the old man stays at the bottom and the new man emerges, free from the past.

In my old church, people used to bring cigarettes, drug paraphernalia, and other things they were bound to with them into the baptismal waters. When they were submerged, they held themselves under for a moment or two and let go of the physical things and the attachments they had to them. A profound understanding existed in this prophetic act, symbolizing all Jesus had accomplished. They were emerging as a new man or woman free from that old sin nature. If we can stop focusing on ourselves and our sin, we may just get free enough to advance His Kingdom.

Filled with the Holy Spirit

In 1987 I was invited to a "secret meeting" with about 12 people from my church who were moving in the gifts of the Spirit. It came after I had been seeking more of Him, searching for an encounter like I read about in so many of the lives of people I admired. I had shifted from thinking there was meant to be no second experience after getting saved to going after anything I could. After we worshiped, the leader asked if anyone would like to be baptized with the Holy Spirit. All eyes looked at me, the only "newbie" in the room. A chair was placed in the middle of the living room and people gathered around me, laid hands on me, and prayed. For the first time in 11 years I began to cry. I tried to make it the "holy cry," the one that is nice, but this was an ugly cry, snot and all. For three days straight I cried. Even when patrolling the streets of Belfast, I would think about Jesus and just start weeping. Since then, I have been prayed for many times, slain in the Spirit, shaken, in a trance, and have had many more experiences, and I would say this: all of them have drawn me closer to Jesus and helped fall more in love with Him.

I don't care if you call it the baptism with, in, or of the Holy Spirit. I don't care if you call it being filled, endued with power from on high, the second blessing, or something else. Just get it and keep getting it.

There is a suggestion from some that we have all of the Holy Spirit and therefore should not ask for more. This ignores the relational aspect of our walk with the Spirit. I have all of my wife and guess what? I want more. I want to experience more of her compassion, more of her laughter. I want to love her more deeply, enjoy more of her company, share my days with her, and spend more time with her. We are by nature called to grow, and any healthy relationship must grow, so why would it be any different in our relationship with the Holy Spirit?

Besides, He is not just filling us for our own sake. He is doing it for the sake of the mission of Jesus and to restore all things. If you say you have enough of Him, show me the signs, wonders, and the Kingdom advancement, and show me how it is growing in you. It is selfish to say, "I have enough." Perhaps it isn't about you.

We have a responsibility to be as drunk (but not as many would suppose) in the Spirit as possible (Acts 2:13-15). Change your thinking, get saved and baptized, and be filled with the Spirit, and you will be positioned to see the Kingdom advance.

What is the Kingdom?

The Kingdom is righteousness, peace, and joy in the Spirit. It's simple. We see the word "righteousness" yet again. Remember, if we see this word and think we must do things better, we are relying on self-righteousness and not His righteousness. We are called to be Holy, not to try to be Holy. So much of the conversation about holiness revolves around us doing things better—not wearing yoga pants, listening to Christian radio, and wondering if Christians can drink or should not drink. These are all good conversations to have, but none of them bring us into more holiness. Holiness is a product of accepting His work for us and that changes us. We don't change to become holy; we become holy and are changed.

Jesus promised us not just peace, but His peace: "My peace I give to you" (John 14:27). This is a peace that goes beyond understanding. It is not based on figuring everything out and rationalizing things: it is a peace that unifies us with the heart of Jesus. It's the same peace Jesus has right now, sitting on His throne. It is an assurance that everything will work out for our good; whatever we have been through can and will be turned to good, and we don't need to fear anything. It is even related to the state of peace we will have when we leave this earth and go to be with Him for eternity.

Like peace, joy is an inside job. I have heard sermons that differentiate between happiness and joy, and I totally get it. I am not happy when bad things happen, I don't feel happy when injustices are unleashed on the earth or when people I love are hurting. I have the ability to mourn with those who mourn. However, it is the joy of the Lord that is my strength—the joy of the One who sits on His throne and laughs. Laughter and joy are some of the biggest weapons in our arsenal for overcoming the lies of the enemy. Lies tell us that we are defeated, we will never have breakthrough, and we will never see the goodness of God in the land of the living. Laughter and joy help us overcome lies by breaking their power and keeping our focus on God. It's in His presence that we experience the fullness of joy (Psalm 16:11). In my life, I have found joy in the darkest of times simply because I believe God to be who He says He is. He is utterly good and is the redeemer of all things.

Talking about the Kingdom can be ineffectual at times. Some think everything they do is "Kingdom." There is of course some truth to this, but it is not necessarily "Kingdom" when I cook, clean, or hang out with friends. Walking down the street is not "Kingdom"; it is merely walking down the street. However, if I do everyday things with the intention of shifting the atmosphere of this world into the atmosphere of heaven, then "Kingdom" becomes possible. It is when we set our minds on things above, not below—an intentional act of bringing the rule of Jesus onto the earth—that the Kingdom is advanced.

At its core, the Kingdom is the restoration of all things. Justice should be seen under a Kingdom lens of restoration. Relationships, ministry, speech, attitudes, and everything else should be viewed with the lens of restoration. Restoration is why miracles, signs, and wonders are possible; it is God's intent to see things as they were originally intended. I believe there will be Kingdom-minded eco-warriors who will begin seeing our planet restored through miracles, signs, and wonders. I believe entrepreneurs will see the economy restored, providing ways for everyone to have enough so that there is no longer poverty among us. I believe God is raising up men and women to speak into family and see families restored, marriages restored, and purity reign. God is raising up Kingdom-minded celebrities, artisans, and performers to proclaim hope, beauty, truth, and His Kingdom come. His Kingdom is radically helpful for everyone on the planet, and we get to do what we love to do and were created for to see it advance.

7

Prophetic Culture

But one who prophesies speaks to men for edification and exhortation and consolation (1 Corinthians 14:3).

Prophecy as it was in the Old Covenant changed with the coming of the New Covenant. It is not the "Old Covenant 2.0," rather it is a New Covenant. What were shadows and types have become the real thing. In the Old Testament, a wrong prophecy could get you killed. Thankfully since the New Covenant, a wrong prophecy means the people around you get to weigh the prophecy.

In the scripture above, you may notice that prophecy is not about judgment, warnings, and exposure. It is for strengthening others, encouraging others, and comforting others. An argument for the prophecy that judges, warns, or exposes goes something along the lines of "By telling them their flaws, I am strengthening them." The problem with this is that accusation, shame, and humiliation are all weapons of a different army. Judgment itself is not the weapon of God—grace and mercy are. This method of "prophecy" risks turning love and all things connected with love into a cold, dispassionate replica of the original for the sake of beating the sheep into conformity. We have been equipped to change all that.

You do not need to be a Christian—let alone filled with the Holy Spirit and moving in the gift of prophecy—to recognize a sinner. Satan does it all the time; he knows our history even when God has chosen to forget it. Calling darkness "light" won't make it any brighter. True light shines in the darkest of places, and we are called to shine to glorify the Father (Matthew 5:16).

Our prophetic culture is connected with our culture of honor. We see the gold in others and search for their heavenly identity, what the Father believes about them. We also fundamentally believe that people change when an internal shift happens, not when external pressure is applied. Calling someone into their God-given identity and purpose allows the individual to make a choice—to pursue who they really are or stay stuck in who they think they are. Prophecy shifts the soul.

Discernment

Prophecy and discernment, along with words of knowledge, are all revelatory gifts of the Spirit. They are gifts of the Spirit. They are not formed by nurture but gifts of the Spirit. Some people have developed a tremendous ability to *read* others, but it is not discernment.

Reading Others

Sam was an alcoholic. He worked at a job where he neither hunted nor gathered—a job where there was neither destiny nor purpose. No future. No hope. What little he received, Sam spent on unholy things, trying to numb the disappointment of his life.

Like many men who worked hard 40 hours a week, he spent Friday evenings at the local pub, magically transforming his paycheck into amber nectar. There was always the hope that this would be the week when those six little numbers Sam chose would metamorphose from his children's birthdates into millions of lottery dollars.

*Each night, the children would try to guess how much amber nectar their father had drunk. One glass was certainly not enough; one bottle would mean certain sleep. It was the amount in between where the great unknown lay. Eight drinks might mean laughter; twelve might mean a release of uncontrollable rage. The children never knew, and they could certainly never ask. Asking "How many whiskeys did you have tonight, Dad?" could lead to a brisk hand across the cheek, or it could mean watching their father, their hero, cry in shame and weakness. So they just had to **know**. It was an unspoken requirement of the family. If one of the children didn't know, he or she was seen as uncaring, inconsiderate, and heartless.*

Sadly, there is no Hollywood ending in the story here. No beauty is rising up from these ashes. Many people grow up in environments similar to this one, in which they must "feel" what is going on in the room in order to survive and keep the peace.

For a seasoned reader who knows how people are doing without ever asking or being told, it can be challenging to walk into a room, even a church sanctuary, and not feel the discord. Seldom do these people feel the joy, but the discord is easy to feel. When we tap into feeling what is happening in heaven and focus on bringing that to earth, joy becomes easy to feel and impart to the room. This shift is one hundred percent obtainable *if* we pursue the gift of discernment and do not rely on the coping skill that we have learned to protect us. Seek the gift, go after what heaven is thinking and a whole new world of peace and joy will open up.

I believe much of what the church has accepted as discernment is actually simply reading others. This skill of reading others is a coping skill, which is not to be confused with the gift of discernment. It is my belief that in its early stages, discernment can look and feel like we are doing what we have learned to do to keep us safe, reading others and our environments. There is one main difference though: using the skills to protect ourselves simply stops at being a coping skill. It does its job well. Discernment, on the other hand, should grow. It should grow into something beautiful and blessed. It's a gift that can see and feel what God is doing. I also believe that some of the most mature "discerners" have started with this ability to read others, but through mastering their own soul and pursuing healing in their lives, they begin to pursue and walk in a God-given gift of discernment.

Resonance

In music, if you have two tuning forks set to the same pitch, when you hit one, the other will resonate and hum simply by responding to what the other is doing. We can understand this concept if we know something about sound waves and forced vibration. I actually think this forced vibration occurs in places outside the physical realm. We often can recognize someone else's emotional pain if it resonates with our own. People who have been abused often recognize others who have been abused. People who are addicts can often "feel" when someone else is an addict. Again, this is not discernment. It is a manifestation of a coping skill at a very basic level. Sadly, the church at large seems to get stuck on defining discernment in this way, which results in people allegedly "discerning" other people's flaws, hurts, and sins.

In all the revelatory gifts, one thing remains central to our growth in them: we must abandon judgment. If we stay in a place of reducing others and believing or seeing only the worst about them, we will simply not grow in our revelation. Potentially even more dangerous is the risk of developing a lens of judgment. Being blocked by a log in our own eye as we try to see the speck in another's will affect the revelation we receive. It is why one prophet sees judgment coming while another sees hope and blessing. Your gift of discernment will manifest whatever is inside you. Your discernment is first and foremost discerning what is inside yourself. You have likely felt yourself reacting to what's happening in other people. Our own inner thoughts and feelings are always the first thing we discern. I would like to write that a hundred times because it is crucial to understand. Growing in discernment is, in the beginning, about acknowledging what you feel is your soul and spirit responding to what is going on around it. Then, as with prophecy, you get to silence that noise and press deeper into what God is doing in the room, the person, or the situation.

I remember going to a conference a few years ago, and I went on my own and vowed I would never go back. I have since repented of that and gone back as I recognized I wasn't practicing what I preach. I didn't want to go back because all I could feel were 800 insecure pastors who needed validation from the "heavyweight" leaders on stage. It felt like there were 800 little Chihuahuas all barking so someone important would notice them. I was asked to run a meeting during this conference to connect people from my region. During the session just before this meeting, I was asked to stand, along with about 20 others, to give people a visual reference of who to follow to each room for the regional meetings. By the end of the day, five people had come to me and given me books they had written. Some of them asked me if I could I pass their books on to the big leaders. All I could see were people who were desperate to connect and be known by "big" Christian leaders. Experiencing this, I felt icky. Do you know why I felt bad? I recognized that I was one of these Chihuahuas too. I had forgotten my own beliefs about discernment, I was feeling my own stuff and it resonated with what was happening inside other people. Instead of mastering me, I had been judging everyone else. To be honest, I ruined my own week.

The biggest safeguard we can have in our gift of discernment is submitting it to authority. This isn't always easy for discerning people because the word "discernment" in Greek means "to know." And if I know something and you disagree, I can easily have the tendency to think you are simply wrong. As with any gift of the Spirit, submitting it to authority is essential. If I am the authority, I need to have someone in my life who can speak truth to me and to whom I will listen to, allowing what is said to influence me. The immature, and sometimes mature, discerner will struggle at times, as I did in the example above. Sometimes we pick things up that are either not ours in the first place, or that are resonating so loudly with issues in our own life that input from others becomes crucial. A lot of people I know who have been hurt by the church are actually incredibly adroit at reading people or may even be discerning, and helping them to understand that what they "know" may not actually be correct can seem impossible. It is the heart of submission, of honor, and knowing who we are that allows discernment to grow.

I think the ability to see in the spirit is a manifestation of the gift of discernment. Even seers need to submit what they see to authority. I know we say that seeing is believing, but seeing is not necessarily the truth. Even our seeing can be from different perspectives. One person may see a blue angel of light and another person may see the same thing as a warrior angel. The gift of seeing is not special enough to be the only gift meant to be used outside of authority and submission. Many years ago, I knew someone who would frequently begin talking to an angel when in a conversation with other people. If you were unaware, you could easily think this person was amazingly spiritual. Instead, he was mentally ill. This was someone who was loved and very loving toward others, and a great person. When confronted, he would submit to an extent but did not really believe that what we were saying was true. He did what we asked but never submitted within his heart. The result was that they left the church, still believing he was right and we were wrong. The problem with deception is that it is deceiving. The biggest safeguard is to be under authority, and nowhere is that more true than with discernment.

Within the DISC assessment that measures the degree of Dominance, Influence, Steadiness, and Conscientiousness in an individual's personality and style, I am a high-D leader. This means I like to lead, am self-confident, a risk taker, and a problem solver. I also have a tendency to be argumentative and not listen well to other opinions. I have worked hard on overcoming these last two. I am not perfect, but I try. Some people "discern" that being self-confident means being arrogant. They have "discerned" that Satan uses people like me to destroy rather than build. In all of this, there have been attempts to turn me into someone else—someone more cuddly. This is not discernment. It is the reaction people have to wounds and hurts of their past as well as their fears of ever being fooled again. I am often told that I remind people of someone in their past who was also a high-D leader, or a cop, or a pastor, or their father—and they "discern" the same thing in me that was characteristic of a person from their past who hurt them. The purpose of discernment isn't to build walls; it is to build bridges between the now and the future—to see what God is doing in all His glory and to bring hope to any situation. Nehemiah knew what his enemy was saying, and knowing this he brought encouragement to his people. It is the job of those who discern to bring encouragement to the people who need it—to those under their watchful care.

I would suggest that the purpose of the watchman in the New Covenant, even though it's never mentioned in the New Testament, is not to see when the enemy is coming or warn of danger, but to look out for what God is about to do and communicate that. Saying the enemy wants to bring a spirit of division in the church is less valuable than saying, "God is bringing an opportunity for His people to unite and be One, and to resist the devil in his attempts to divide."

There are times when God does warn us, but it is always redemptive. Telling a person, city, or nation they are about to face calamity and saying it's because of their disobedience without offering some hope doesn't sound like the Spirit of God. The message from the watchmen must be one of hope, not destruction.

Often people will discern and even see the demonic, and this is especially true of kids. Remember it is how I got started. There are some things that may help with this. We often first see or discern what is in us manifesting as things around us. In other words, if our life is filled with fear, we will probably always discern or see the dark side of the spiritual realm. If our life is filled with hope, we will discern the light side. Hebrews 5:14 tells us specifically that we must train our senses to discern, yet most of us have not trained our senses, so we think anything that comes through them must be true. It says, *"But solid food is for the mature, who because of practice have their senses trained to discern good and evil."*

The same word for "discern" is used here as in 1 Corinthians, but most notable in this verse is the word "practice." This passage is saying we need to take our gift to the gym! This is not going for a run ourselves; rather it is training with others under the supervision of an instructor at a gym. How many have left the church and become ineffective because they failed to train their senses and instead got carried away by their commitment to being right and independent?

I do something called CrossFit. Google it and you will find stories of injuries, often resulting from bad coaching or people trying to do the exercises on their own. Doing it after reading articles, books, and watching some YouTube videos is a disaster waiting to happen. How well I do at the gym is about two things: (1) the quality of instruction and (2) leaving my ego at the door. If you want to grow in discernment, get some quality instruction from someone who actually discerns and isn't just suspicious of people (especially people who have hurt them in the past). Also, leave your spiritual ego at the door. You will get it wrong at times, and you will need to correct things and adjust yourself and your gift to be able to discern better and grow in your gift.

With all these gifts, please remember that if you can speak in the tongues of men and angels, if you prophesy knowing all mysteries and knowledge, but do not have love, it is worthless (1 Corinthians 13:1–2). You get no points for that. My wife teaches our church in the prophetic. She has beginner, intermediate, and advanced classes, and leads a School of Emerging Prophets. She does a fantastic job at instilling our values deep into the prophetic training. Do you want to know what our Advanced Prophecy module is based on? The Father's love. If love is not at the core of what we do and how we operate, then we have wasted our time. Neither you nor I get to define love. Paul did it for us, and while it is used a lot in weddings, the context is how we do church and the life in the Spirit.

Love never gives up.

Love cares more for others than for self.

Love doesn't want what it doesn't have.

Love doesn't strut,

Doesn't have a swelled head,

Doesn't force itself on others,

Isn't always "me first,"

Doesn't fly off the handle,

Doesn't keep score of the sins of others,

Doesn't revel when others grovel,

Takes pleasure in the flowering of truth,

Puts up with anything,

Trusts God always,

Always looks for the best,

Never looks back,

But keeps going to the end (1 Corinthians 13:4–7 The Message).

Our entire prophetic culture is based on these verses. Love has been replaced sometimes with being right and with anger at social injustices. If you want to move in God's great power displayed by prophecy, miracles, and righting the wrongs of society, it must come second to walking in love. I may be walking a tightrope here, but love must be known as love, not anger. If the other party is hurt and upset when you don't agree with him or her, the culture of honor comes into play. Our goal, even in the revelatory gifts, is to stay connected.

We teach that with all revelation there are three things requiring prayer, wisdom, and input. The first is the revelation itself. Whether it's a picture, internally hearing God, feeling something, or just knowing something, the revelation will require input. Sometimes this can be just sharing it with the person it's for, in the company of another, and simply asking them if it means anything. Then interpretation is needed. If you see a dollar sign over someone, it does not mean they are wealthy. It could mean they're in debt or in the financial industry. It could also mean they should go into the financial industry or stay away from that type of work. How do you know? Go to the prophetic gym. Get trained on how to interpret prophetic words by an experienced prophet. My wife does exercises at all her trainings. They start easy but become progressively more difficult. Oftentimes people make mistakes, but they also get better—more sculpted in their gift. You need a safe place to practice, with safe people, and you need to be secure enough to be wrong and get adjusted. This is how you will lift heavier prophetic weights!

Second comes the application. This is one place where people need a lot of help. In this part of prophecy, it's so easy to place my hopes and dreams and my fears and insecurities onto the interpretation of the word. I have seen people receive a revelation about finances coming and abundance coming, and they have immediately bought a big house, a boat, and a car. Of course the finances don't typically come through immediately, and they end up in debt and foreclosure, become skeptical of prophecy, and feel disconnected from God. The problem is not with the revelation or interpretation; it is with the application. If God calls you to be a prophet, don't get your business cards printed immediately. Learn to apply the Word of God well. Get trained and come under an established prophet. Be humble and learn all you can. Don't limit the process of growing and making progress.

On December 27, 1980, I asked God to show me who I was going to marry. I was 16 and had only been saved for seven months. I didn't even believe in prophecy. I really liked a girl and hoped it would be her. I knew I could be courageous enough to ask her out if God would speak and tell me it was her. But I felt God say to me that the next girl who walked around the corner would be my wife. I thought this was absurd. I was in the center of Belfast and it was two days after Christmas, so the streets were filled with shoppers returning gifts. Just then, a girl walked around the corner and it was someone I knew. She was *way* out of my league. You know that girl you don't even consider because every guy has a thing for her? I had only met her a couple of times and thought she was nice, but there was nothing more, no spark, no "vavavoom," simply because she was way too gorgeous to be interested in me. We said hello to each other, exchanged pleasantries, and moved on. I told God that was crazy. I could never see a girl like that going for me. And God told me right then and there that I would have to wait seven years for the girl He had shown me.

Over the next few months, my heart started to shift. I wanted to be near this girl, I wanted to know more about her, and when we hung out, I really enjoyed her company. She was the most encouraging and beautiful person I had ever met. We used to walk to a Bible study together and this became the most precious time of my week. But could I really believe she would marry me? And would it really be seven years? If this was true, then I didn't want to date anyone in the meantime, so I needed to know. Each time I spoke to the Lord about her, He said, "She is the one."

Somehow I knew that going to her and saying, "The Lord has ordained us to marry each other and you will be in direct disobedience to the will of God if you refuse" was a bad idea. So, like Mary the mother of Jesus, I kept these things and pondered them in my heart.

There were times when I wondered if it would happen. I would hear that she was dating a guy, and do you know what I did? I prayed for the success and health of their relationship. I knew that if this was truly God, "we" would happen. Don't get me wrong, I was devastated when she dated someone else, but I never wanted "us" to happen by my strength or power, but by the Spirit. During times when I doubted, I would ask God for confirmation. Each time, He gave it. I remained resolute. All my friends knew how I felt about her. Some would caution me to be sensible; others told me to be obedient. My pastor, who loved me and was skeptical, said I should wait and see. Others said I should ignore the timing thing—and just go for it and ask her out.

The reality is that we both needed the time. I needed the time to mature. I would spend months head over heels in love, and months feeling nothing, glad to be single. When I bought my own house at 22 years old, I thought, "Thank God I am not dating, or worse still, married." I had the opportunity to learn so much about love and how it's not a feeling. To cut a long story short: seven years and one month after God spoke to me (after an attempt at dating each other that was a disaster), we started dating. That was in January 1988, and we got married in March 1989. She is the only woman I have ever loved. I am so thankful for the revelation, the interpretation, but most importantly the application of what God promised. I waited, received counsel, prayed, fasted, got confirmations, and worked on my maturity. I sometimes cannot believe that I have this marriage that is simply wonderful. It all came from asking—and when I asked, I believed.

When Rachel and I moved to the USA, people wanted to know the story of how God called us here. We had stories of visas coming through in weeks rather than months, Rachel's business being blessed so we could pay off debts, our house getting rented easily, and more. Touching foot on U.S. soil was a different thing altogether. It was not an easy transition, everything was a battle, and we had to contend for almost everything in that season. Many of us see smooth sailing, with the occasional curve ball, as an indication we are in the will of God. We look to counsel and circumstances. We look to opposition to tell us if we are on the right course. This must stop. Either God said it or He didn't, and once we decide that He said it, we hold on to it like our lives depend on it.

The disciples who panicked in the storm while Jesus slept were not rebuked for their lack of faith because they did not command the storm to cease. Their lack of faith was evident in their not believing when Jesus said, "We are going to the other side" that He meant it and was content to sleep no matter what storm there was (Mark 4:35–41). When we have a sense of God's direction or when we get a prophecy, we often use the "peace" test. "Do you have peace about it?" This is a pretty useless question in my mind. It's an indication of our comfort level about a decision, not God's hand in it. To reiterate, smooth sailing is not an indication of God's will.

Moses, David, Jacob, Abraham, Paul, Timothy, Peter—name a biblical hero and you will see opposition and storms. There were delays and testing of their faith to believe that what God said would come to pass. God uses prophecy to make us aware of things in our hearts that perhaps we didn't even know existed, and He uses prophecy to create realities that are not yet there. We are pulled into our future through prophecy.

If I receive a prophecy that says I will go to the nations and sit with kings, and I then take that prophecy to a counselor who tells me to do x, y, or z with it, I do not receive the prophet's reward. I will probably get good counsel—but not the reward of the prophet. The first thing I must do to receive the reward is to determine the answer to three simple questions: (1) Is this from God? (2) Is God speaking through this? (3) Am I receiving this as an actual prophecy? Once I answer these, I no longer have an option whether or not to obey. Receiving the prophecy as being from God removes the option to obey or not obey, even if that means I am shipwrecked. Most "good" counsel would have told Paul to quit. One shipwreck is bad enough, but three? God must be telling you something!

One effect of a prophecy is that it tests you. *"Until the time that his word came to pass, the word of the Lord tested him"* (Psalm 105:19). It was a prophetic dream that tested Joseph. He was beaten by his brothers, placed in shackles, became a slave, and thrown in prison. And he overcame it all. Prophecy, when accepted as prophecy, has the power to overcome. But to overcome means there is something that will need to be overcome. The reward of treating prophecy as prophecy is that it will endure if we are courageous and do not lose faith.

In Luke 22:31, Jesus tells Peter what is about to happen:

"Simon, Simon, behold, Satan has demanded permission to sift you like wheat; but I have prayed for you, that your faith may not fail; and you, when once you have turned again, strengthen your brothers." Peter tells Jesus he is willing to be imprisoned and even die, two things that would later come true. But at this point, Peter was about to fail miserably. Jesus did not pray that Peter would not fail. He prayed that Peter's faith wouldn't fail so that when he returned to do what he had been called to do, he would do it and strengthen others.

When God speaks a word, and once we acknowledge it is from God and see that it has a proper interpretation and a good application, then we are responsible for our obedience to it. This is true no matter what happens. If God has decreed that you will be married, no age or lack of opportunity will undermine the word promised. If God has decreed your healing, no setbacks or lab results will determine your health. If God has decreed your finances will be healthy, no bank statement will set the course of your abundance. If God has called you to go to the nations, no act of man will thwart the will of God. What He decrees, He fulfills. I would rather die believing than live in unbelief. (Of course, I would rather live believing than die believing, but you get my point.)

However, we can choose to disobey a word. We can see the storms as evidence of the word not really being from God and move from receiving it as a prophecy, to seeing it as a whim of our heart. We can chose comfort, and comfort is the enemy of persistence, endurance, and ultimately fulfilled prophecy.

Our prophetic words often carry with them tests, and most of the time, a test is probably not going to be something that's completed within an afternoon. We see in the lives of many that testing can last for years. When I say testing, I don't mean things are delayed. I mean things are apparently moving in the opposite direction.

You have a call and a destiny. It has been tested. The test is not for your character; it is so that once you have failed, been disappointed, denied what you are called to do, made mistakes, and even made deliberate acts that conflict with your call and destiny, your faith in the word God has given you will remain intact. Your responsibility in all of this is to have a decided heart. We need a heart that is aligned with God and won't be moved once it knows His will. Some people fail at whatever they attempt because of an undecided, wavering heart. In *The Seven Decisions*, author Andy Andrews says, "When confronted with a challenge, the committed heart will search for a solution. The undecided heart searches for an escape." We cannot interpret prophecy intellectually—we must do it in our hearts and be fully committed once we know.

The apostle Paul said he wishes we all moved in prophecy. The prophetic has the ability to change people, communities, and cities. But it requires a people who are ready to stand, believe in the goodness of God, and have the perseverance of warriors who not only fight, but fight so hard their hands freeze to their swords.

Conclusion

This book began as a way to clarify our core values for people new to Greater Chicago Church. Then others began asking for it, and so it has developed into this. I am fairly confident I will need to add to it as time goes on. I, like the apostle Paul, am sure I have not arrived, but I continue to run this race. And I will grow and learn as I go.

We have developed weekend intensives around each of these seven core values. These intensives are designed to help individuals and churches embrace a culture that I am convinced is needed more than ever in these glorious days.

My life is dedicated to raising sons and daughters who can answer the moaning of all creation and show up in their lives as Kingdom people, a people who will win cities and father nations for the Glory of our Father, for Jesus to receive the rewards of His sufferings, and for the Spirit to be poured out on all flesh.

Beannaithe,

Ian